Seahorses

Everything About History, Care,
Nutrition, Handling, and Behavior

Filled with Full-color Photographs
and Illustrations

BARRON'S

2 CONTENTS

CLASSIFICATION AND CHARACTERISTICS

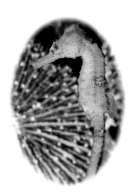

Taxonomists have been bedeviled by seahorses' appearance for ages. Even the great Carolus Linnaeus, the father of modern taxonomy, mistakenly classified them as amphibians. The genus name, Hippocampus, is derived from the Greek words for horse/sea monster, and it is little wonder that they are so described.

General Classification

The bizarre appearance of the seahorse has given rise to tales of mythical creatures bearing sea gods upon their backs. Their horse's head, armadillo's armor, monkey's tail, opossum's pouch, independently moving eyes, and wing-like fins have led taxonomists to ascribe the seahorse to all manner of animal families.

Seahorses are true bony fish, as is the tuna. However, their mystique remains. They are assigned to the family Syngnathidae (from the Greek, meaning "fused jaws"), along with the pipefish, pipe horses, and sea dragons. The family is placed within the order Syngnathi-formes (or Gasterosteiformes), which includes the sea moths (Pegasidae), trumpet fish (Aulastomidae), ghost pipefish (Solenostomidae), coronet fish (Fistulariidae), razor fish (Centriscidae), paradox fish (Indostomidae), and the bellows fish (Macrorhamphosidae).

A brilliantly colored slender seahorse (H. reidi).

Over 120 species of seahorse have been described. However, a recent review by S. A. Laurie (see Information, page 91) indicates that these may be condensed to 32 species. Of course, undescribed species likely abound. Classification is complicated because individuals of the same species can change color to match their background and can grow filamentous appendages (cirri) that help with camouflage. Of particular trouble to aquarists is the name thorny seahorse, *Hippocampus histrix*, being applied to several Indo-Pacific species with spinelike projections, and the name yellow seahorse, *H. kuda*, which is also applied to any smooth seahorse from the same region.

Characteristics

Locomotion: Seahorses' mode of locomotion is as unusual as their appearance. The animals are propelled entirely by the beating of the small dorsal fin. They use the tiny pectoral fins, high up on the head, for steering. Despite the

6

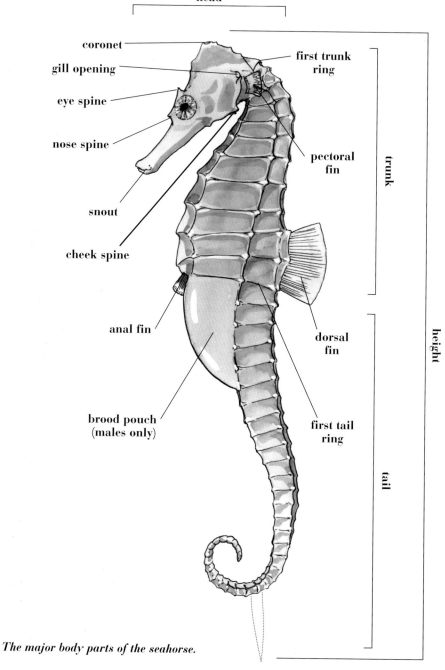

head

coronet

gill opening

eye spine

nose spine

snout

cheek spine

anal fin

brood pouch
(males only)

first trunk
ring

pectoral
fin

dorsal
fin

first tail
ring

trunk

tail

height

The major body parts of the seahorse.

inability to generate power with the tail (it lacks a caudal fin), seahorses can attain respectable speeds, for short distances, by beating the dorsal fin up to 75 times per second. An upper limit upon speed is imposed by the bony plates that cover the body and prevent it from flexing. The fluttering motion of the dorsal and pectoral fins gave rise to the stories that seahorses "flew" through the water on wings.

The tail: Although the tail is barely used in locomotion, it is long, prehensile, and extremely important to a seahorse's lifestyle. By using the tail, these weak swimmers can nonetheless survive in areas of waves and strong currents by remaining anchored to plants or other stable items in the environment. By blending in well with these holdfasts, the seahorses can feed on small creatures brought to them by the water's flow. Seahorses' eyes move independently, like a chameleon, and allow the animals to take full advantage of their sedentary existence. The tail also functions in mating, pair greetings, and male wrestling matches.

Body shape and color: A body disrupted by spines and fleshy appendages (cirri), along with a well-developed ability to change color, gives these unique beasts an extra degree of camouflage. In some species, the cirri can be grown as needed. So highly developed is their color-changing ability that they can reach even extremes of orange and red when necessary. This ability helps seahorses to catch food and avoid enemies because, despite the protective body armor, a variety of fish and crabs feed on them. Color change is probably also a form of communication, as in cuttlefish, octopuses, and many lizards. Such changes may indicate aggression, state of health, recognition, or a variety of as yet unknown states of being. The head is topped by a bony growth known as the coronet, which varies in shape from species to species.

Seahorses, to the surprise of many aquarists and divers, can make clicking noises by grinding certain skull bones together. The role that these sounds play in seahorse ecology is not yet understood.

Distribution and Habitat

Although often thought of as tropical fish, seahorses actually range throughout the world's oceans. The long-snouted seahorse, *H. guttulatus*, lives as far north as northern Norway. Several other species occur as far south as southern New Zealand. The waters they inhabit range in temperature from 42.8°F to 86°F (6°C to 30°C). Seahorses do, however, reach their greatest diversity in the warm waters of the Indo-Pacific. Ten species are found off Australia, while only one inhabits the cold waters of the northwest Atlantic Ocean.

Although seahorses are strictly marine fish, many live in estuaries and deal with fluctuating salinity. The Kynsna seahorse, *H. capensis*, is found in south African estuaries where the water's salt content may rise from its normal 3.5 percent to 40 percent. (Seahorse mortality does occur during periods of heavy freshwater inundation.) Some species of the seahorse's close relative, the pipefish, do inhabit freshwater.

Seahorses are, for the most part, creatures of shallow coastline habitats. However, they are occasionally encountered many miles out to sea and have been caught in fishing nets set at depths of 541 feet (165 m). They probably

*The small dorsal fin provides locomotion (northern seahorse, **H. erectus**).*

traveled while attached to floating plants, as seahorses are not distance swimmers.

The habitats in which seahorses live are among the earth's most productive and, consequently, vital to both people and millions of other species. Sadly, these habitats are also among those most prone to human disturbance (see page 89). Sea grass beds (meadows of flowering marine plants), mangrove forests (stands of mud-stabilizing trees with aerial roots), coral reefs (structures composed of the hard skeletons of tiny marine animals), and estuaries (areas where freshwater rivers empty into the sea) comprise the earth's most biologically diverse habitats. These are the haunts of most of the world's seahorse species. Efforts to protect these areas will benefit humankind, seahorses, and other species. Conservation efforts aimed specifically at seahorses should also be of advantage to their habitats.

Surprises concerning habitat choice continue to arise as more is learned about seahorses in the wild. For example, the pygmy seahorse, *H. bargibanti*, has been found on only two species of soft coral (gorgonian), and it so closely matches these that the species was not discovered until the soft corals had been collected and placed into an aquarium.

Feeding Behavior

All aspects of seahorses are unique—including their feeding behavior. Seahorses in the wild appear to hunt strictly by sight and will take only moving prey. The main food of most species appears to be small shrimps and other crustaceans, but they will accept other foods in captivity (see page 45). Much is still not known about their natural diet.

TIP

Day or Night?

Seahorses are generally more active by day than by night. However, the tiger-tail seahorse, *H. comes*, and the Pacific seahorse, *H. ingens*, appear to be nocturnal.

More unique is the seahorses' method of capturing meals. When prey is sighted by the eyes (which move independently), a seahorse usually remains anchored to its holdfast by its tail and stretches toward its victim. The animal's head flicks, and the prey is sucked through the long, tubular snout. The narrow mouth cavity is enlarged by the retraction of a small bone, known as the hyoid, and a dropping of the lower jaw. This motion also helps enhance the work of a small siphon at the top of the gills, which concentrates and expels water from the snout. The two siphon holes can be observed at the top of the sea-horse's head.

Seahorses lack teeth, but the food is often shredded by its passage through the thin snout. The digestive tract is simple and lacks a stomach. Food passes through rapidly and is often excreted in a partially digested state. Partly as a result of this anatomic arrangement,

A seahorse consuming a brine shrimp.

*Seahorses rely mainly upon camouflage for protection (yellow seahorse, **H. kuda**).*

seahorses must consume huge quantities of food, which complicates their captive husbandry. Their appearance and lifestyle combine to render them extremely efficient hunters. Fry have been observed to consume nearly 4,000 brine shrimps per day, and adults of many species catch at least 50 food items daily.

Reproduction

Seahorses reach their extremes in outlandish behavior in the area of reproduction, testing the very limits of what is possible. The male undergoes a true pregnancy. The female produces the eggs, but the male carries them in a special pouch on the underside of the tail. Embryos embed in the pouch's epithelial tissue, and oxygen is supplied by capillaries. The male does not appear to provide nourishment to the young. However, he does contribute calcium and alters the chemical composition of the pouch fluids according to the embryos' needs.

Pair-bonds: Seahorses—at least those studied thus far—are also unusual in forming exclusive pair-bonds, possibly for life. Pairs have been observed to stay together even when no young are produced after copulation. Single animals typically take a long time to find a new mate if one dies. Many species appear to reinforce this bond with a highly stylized greeting ceremony that is performed throughout the breeding season. The female initiates this ritual by entering the male's territory, usually in the morning. Both animals may then change to a different (usually lighter) color, and the male circles the female. The two then spiral about a common holdfast for up to an hour, and the pair does not separate until the next morning. This elaborate ceremony may be necessary to ensure that both sexes are ready to mate at the same time, as timing is essential in seahorse reproduction. This is because the female must add water to her eggs shortly before mating to insure fertilization. However, she is able to hold these hydrated eggs for only 24 hours. If the male cannot accept them during this period, they are released into the sea and fail to hatch.

Actual courtship can be lengthy—up to ten hours in certain species. It involves spiraling in a manner similar to that of the morning greeting and swimming about with tails interlocked. Just prior to mating, both rise toward the surface, and the male pumps his tail toward his body, forcing water in and out of the pouch. At this point, the female aligns her egg duct, or ovipositor, with the male's pouch and transfers her egg strands. Egg output varies greatly. The tiny pygmy seahorse lays but one or two, while males of the big-bellied seahorse, *H. abdominalis*, have been known to carry 1,500. The male's subsequent rocking motions seem designed to settle the eggs into place.

The eggs are incubated anywhere from six days to six weeks, depending upon the species and the temperature of the water. Tail

A female seahorse (on the right) transferring eggs to the male's pouch.

thrusting by the male can last for several hours. It forcibly ejects the tiny fry, which are 0.2 to 0.5 inch (6 to 12 mm) in length. The newborns are minute versions of the adults, although the body proportions are different. In some species, the young drift about the sea for some time, while others attach to plants and take up the adult lifestyle immediately. Little is known about the effects that drifting has upon dispersal and the colonization of new areas.

Both sexes compete for mates. However, only males have been seen to tail wrestle or to flick their heads at each other in aggressive encounters.

Seahorses living in temperate areas, such as the northern, or Atlantic, seahorse (*H. erectus*) have a seasonally limited breeding season. In contrast, tropical species may be influenced by seasonal rains or may reproduce year-round.

Territorial and Activity Patterns

Little is known about the home ranges of most species. The females of those that have been studied occupy territories of up to 15 square feet (1.4 sq m). These overlap the smaller, 6-square-foot (0.5-sq-m) territories of their mates. Many species of seahorse appear to exhibit long-term site fidelity, but competition for space has not been observed. The pair forages separately during the day, joining only at the morning greeting or during actual copulation.

Temperate species abandon their feeding and mating grounds during the winter. They apparently spend this time in deeper water. However, the details of this behavior, and how or if pair-bonds are maintained, is unknown.

Choosing a Species

Research, and not availability, should be your guide when choosing a seahorse species. The fact that a seahorse is offered for sale, even on a regular basis, is absolutely no guarantee that its husbandry needs are understood. Many species are collected from the wild in great numbers and perish rapidly in captivity, only to be replaced by other wild-collected specimens.

The climate in which you live and your average home temperature are important factors to consider when purchasing a seahorse. Heating an aquarium is generally easier than cooling one. Therefore, aquarists living in warm climates should not choose a species from a cold-water environment. You must also take into account your finances. Heating and cooling costs add greatly to the overall expense of maintaining a seahorse aquarium.

Ready access to marine environments is crucial if you plan to collect live food for your seahorses. Because of the paucity of appropriate food sources, living near a marine environment can almost be considered a prerequisite for successfully keeping all but a few seahorse species. Likewise, choosing a species that is native to your area will help you provide some of the foods on which the animal feeds. Native species are also recommended because providing them with a natural light cycle is easier. This is easily arranged by locating the aquarium near a window. Such a situation will encourage reproduction, especially if combined with appropriate temperature fluctuations.

The feeding requirements of larger species are, in general, easier to accommodate than are those of smaller seahorses. This is true mainly because a wider variety of food items can be consumed due to the size of the mouth

Be sure to do some research before choosing a seahorse species for your home aquarium.

The seahorse uses its long snout to capture small sea creatures (thorny seahorse, **H. hystrix***).*

and snout. One exception is the dwarf seahorse, *H. zosterae*, which seems to fare well on a diet of nutritionally supplemented brine shrimps.

A key to maintaining seahorses in captivity is inducing the animals to accept nonliving food items. This allows a wide variety of nutritionally supplemented items to be included in the diet without the daunting task of maintaining food animals at home. The northern seahorse,

H. erectus, and the black seahorse, *H. fuscus*, are two species that take to dead food fairly readily. Please note, however, that individuals within both species may not accept nonliving food items.

Please always choose a seahorse species that is being bred in captivity as opposed to one collected from the wild. Not only will you be making an environmentally sound decision, but you are also more likely to obtain a healthier

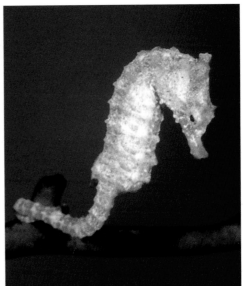

*The dwarf seahorse is the only species that
does well on a "brine shrimp only" diet.*

animal that will adapt well to aquarium life.
Responsible breeders will also be able to provide you with a wealth of information about
the species and individual animals that you
purchase.

*The large snout of the northern seahorse
allows it to take a wide variety of prey.*

Searching for the Right One

Once you have decided on an appropriate species of seahorse, you can begin searching for a healthy, well-established individual. Retail pet stores can be a source of specimens but only if you are certain that the owner or salesperson will answer your questions knowledgeably and truthfully. Aquarium magazines and local aquarium societies are an excellent source of animals. These will more likely be sources of captive-bred specimens, and you will be able to avail yourself of a breeder's expertise. No amount of research can replace a conversation with a person who has bred and cared for the animal in which you are interested. The Internet has opened a vast new avenue of commerce in seahorses, but as with pet stores, please use caution.

When examining a prospective seahorse for your aquarium, try to observe the animal for as long as possible. Of particular importance is that you see the animal feeding. Do not consider purchasing a seahorse that refuses food. Determining whether or not a seahorse has been feeding over time takes a bit of practice. The skin between the body ridges should be even with the ridges or should bulge out slightly. Nongravid females will have a depressed area extending for four to five segments but should otherwise appear as described above.

Healthy seahorses that are not hunting will generally be anchored to a holdfast. Animals that swim about constantly or sway listlessly near the bottom are likely stressed and are not good candidates for your aquarium. Review the section about health (page 53), and bear in mind the signs of illness in seahorses. Be particularly sure

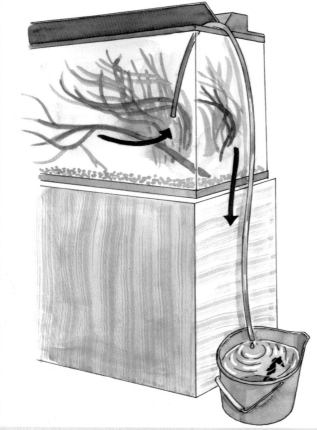

Use a slow drip when transfering aquarium water to the bucket.

that the eyes are clear and that the seahorse appears alert. Check for signs of fungus (dark film) or parasitic infection (white or yellow spots) as well as for wounds. Frayed fins and missing tail tips are also danger signals. Fins may regrow. However, fraying may be a sign of bacterial infection, and wounds are a potential site for such.

Pay attention to the condition of the aquarium in which the seahorse lives. Avoid purchasing animals held in obviously dirty or poorly maintained enclosures. Review the section about setting up an aquarium (page 25). A poorly designed aquarium may indicate that the retailer lacks the basic knowledge required to keep seahorses properly. Such a person is likely to have made mistakes that could severely jeopardize the health of the animals being offered for sale. Obtain details about the food the seahorse accepts. Also ask to take temperature, salinity, and pH readings. You will need these to acclimate the seahorse to your aquarium successfully. Do not purchase seahorses from retailers who refuse to allow you to take these readings. If the readings are within acceptable limits but differ from those in your aquarium, ask the retailer to include a gallon or so of water from the seahorse's current aquarium. This will help with the acclimation process.

Acclimating the Seahorse to Your Aquarium

If the temperature and pH of your aquarium closely match those of the aquarium in which the seahorse had been housed, the acclimation process is as follows:

1. Shut off the aquarium lights.

2. Float the bag containing the seahorse in your aquarium for 10 minutes.

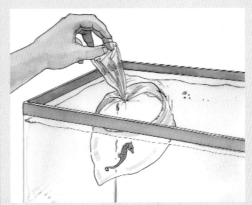

The proper way to acclimate your seahorse to an aquarium.

3. Add a small amount of water from your aquarium to the bag containing the seahorse.

4. Continue adding a bit of water every 15 minutes for 45 minutes.

5. Release the seahorse into your aquarium.

If the temperature and pH in your aquarium vary widely from that of the retailer, place the seahorse and its water into a clean bucket near your aquarium. Using a length of air line tubing, allow water to drip from your aquarium into the bucket containing the seahorse. Plastic valves that allow you to control the speed of water flow are available at pet stores. Alternatively, you can use a variety of binder clips or paper clips. Take temperature and pH readings after 20 minutes, and adjust the flow accordingly. Ideally, the readings should approach each other within one hour's time. Because the seahorse will remain in the bucket for a long time, be sure to include an appropriate anchorage site and some plastic plants as cover. Transfer the seahorse into your aquarium when the temperature and pH levels equalize. Be sure to check the level of water in the bucket regularly to avoid overflowing it.

AQUARIUM HABITATS FOR CAPTIVE SEAHORSES

Aquariums for keeping marine creatures must be made of glass or acrylic because the metal in framed models will leach toxins into the water. Acrylic tanks are lighter than glass and offer rounded front panels. However, they scratch easily and are expensive. All-glass aquariums can be had in an almost unlimited variety of sizes and shapes, and they are the most commonly used vessels.

Types of Aquariums

The location of the aquarium will be your first consideration. An often-overlooked concern is the aquarium's weight. A 55-gallon (200-L) tank with water and gravel weighs in excess of 600 pounds (270 kg), so be sure that your floorboards and aquarium stand are adequate. Positioning the aquarium near a window (but not in direct sunlight) will assist in establishing a day/night cycle that coincides with local conditions. (You can also accomplish this with light timers.) Be sure that the aquarium is not in direct sunlight for the entire day, as algae and heat buildup may become a problem. If the seahorses you keep are from an area with a seasonal cycle similar to your own, then such placement will help maintain normal activity levels and may encourage breeding.

Seahorses are best maintained in complex, naturalistic aquariums.

IMPORTANT NOTE

Seahorses and their relatives are among the most difficult of all creatures to maintain, let alone breed, in captivity. This is the case even for experienced professionals at major public aquariums, so the private hobbyist must think long and hard before seeking to obtain these animals. If your attempts to keep them in captivity are unsuccessful, please resist the temptation to purchase additional animals until you have discovered the reasons for their failure to thrive.

Size: A marine aquarium, even one housing relatively sessile fish such as seahorses, must be larger than a freshwater aquarium with a similar number of inhabitants. In general, avoid anything less than 20 gallons (75 L), and start with a 40-gallon (150-L) aquarium if possible.

Undetected changes in pH, temperature, and ammonia levels are much less serious in a large tank. Even one pair of seahorses requires more room than most aquarists can provide. Normal behavior and reproduction can, and indeed usually must, occur within enclosures that do not approach the size of normal territories. However, your animals will always fare better when given as much space as possible. Fewer animals in a large, well-planted aquarium will absolutely provide more enjoyment, and be healthier, than those that are crowded. Oddly enough, animals will not get lost in a large tank but will actually show themselves much more, and in a more natural manner, than if they are crowded.

The shape of your aquarium should be long and low. These tanks provide more surface area and more of the type of space required by seahorses than do shorter, deeper ones. Beware of oddly shaped designer aquariums. Many are interesting to look at but provide little usable space and limited surface area for oxygen exchange. They are best reserved for use with less delicate animals or species requiring oddly shaped enclosures. For instance, tall, octogonal tanks are ideal for tree frogs and burrowing tarantulas, but not for seahorses.

Mixed-Species Aquariums

The slow, methodical swimming and hunting style of seahorses limits the type of creatures that you may safely house with them. Almost any fish that feeds upon live food will outcompete the seahorses and will probably harass the seahorses by nipping at them. The dual stress of low food intake and aggression will quickly cause your pets' demise. Very small, bottom-dwelling fish such as tiny flounders, blennies, and gobies may be tried. Pipefish will also coexist peaceably. The author was able to maintain a pair of four spined sticklebacks with seahorses, but great attention was required as to food intake.

Invertebrates offer greater potential as seahorse companions. Small hermit crabs and spider crabs (but not other crab species), shrimps (although not aggressive species such as mantis shrimps), snails, starfish, and marine worms all work well. If you are able to meet their special needs, you can also add filtered feeding invertebrates such as various mollusks and corals.

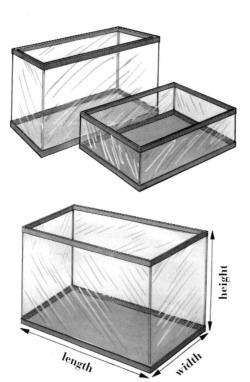

Glass aquariums come in a variety of shapes and sizes.

If you are new to keeping seahorses, please begin with only the seahorses. Add other creatures as you gain experience. For a more detailed discussion of other suitable tankmates, see page 82. *The Marine Aquarium Handbook* (see Information, page 91) provides excellent information about caring for some of these marine arthropods and other invertebrates.

Quarantine and Hospital Aquariums

If you add new animals to your aquarium, establish a quarantine tank to house them for the first month or so. This will allow you to monitor the animals closely for signs of illness and for their feeding preferences. Please be aware that seahorses have a very specific social structure. Any new tankmates can be a source of stress.

A separate, filtered aquarium should always be running and ready to accept sick animals. This step will be worth its expense and trouble when an animal falls ill, as anyone who has tried to set up an aquarium on a moment's notice will attest. A pair of black mollies can be kept in the aquarium during vacancies to assist in normal nutrient cycling (see page 25).

The Nursery Aquarium

Water quality: The enormous food requirements of baby seahorses (up to 3,000 food items per day!) necessitates that they be constantly surrounded by food. The main concern (aside from obtaining so much food) is poor water quality caused by uneaten food organisms that die in the aquarium. This is especially true when using freshwater invertebrates, such as rotifers, which expire quickly in salt water.

You should also bear in mind that young seahorses produce a great deal of waste material despite their small size, and they grow rapidly during their first year.

Filtration: Dead food animals should be siphoned from the aquarium several times each day. The siphoning process can also serve as a partial water change, which is of particular importance in maintaining water quality. Filtration must be mild so that the weakly swimming seahorses can move about easily and catch food. A sponge filter attached to a small air pump is particularly useful since it is less likely to suck up food animals. If this still occurs, decrease the pump's power with a bleeder valve. To clean the sponge filter, squeeze it in a bucket of salt water—washing under hot tap water will kill the beneficial bacteria. The high biological load in the nursery aquarium and the lack of chemical filtration mean that frequent partial water changes must be performed. Seahorses are best raised in bare-bottomed aquariums since they can more easily find food in this situation. This also simplifies cleaning. As they mature and are feeding well on larger food items, the young seahorses can be switched to an aquarium that uses an undergravel filter.

Aquarium Furnishings

The major furnishings of the aquarium, such as rocks, corals, and plants, must be chosen to provide your seahorses with the security conducive to a stress-free existence.

Rocks are useful in creating sight barriers within the aquarium. Do not collect rocks because even those taken from the sea can leach harmful chemicals. Several types, such

Above: Coral skeletons and sea fans are
favored anchorage sites.

A thorny seahorse (Hippocampus hystrix).

Learn to recognize the hallmarks of a
healthy specimen.

Larger seahorses will use sea cactus as anchorage sites.

CHECKLIST

Checklist of Aquarium Supplies
✔ Substrate
- crushed coral
- seashells
- dolomite

✔ Rock
✔ Live rock
✔ Water
- artificial
- natural

✔ Coral
- replicas
- skeletons
- live coral

✔ Plants
- replicas
- living marine algae

✔ Nitrifying bacteria or a "starter" fish
✔ Hydrometer
✔ Thermometer
✔ Heater
✔ pH test kit
✔ Ammonia/nitrite test kit
✔ Aquarium cover and light
✔ Filters
- biological
- mechanical
- chemical

✔ Gravel washer
✔ Glass cleaner

mollusks, and other creatures. Live rock can be an important filtration mechanism (see page 35) as well as a decoration.

Coral skeletons make excellent anchorage sites for seahorses. Collecting them, however, has caused ecological havoc and is prohibited in the United States, Australia, and other countries. If you choose to use natural coral, use only farmed coral. (Such farms are operating in Indonesia and the Solomon Islands.)

Coral already in your possession should be cleaned because even long-dead pieces may harbor harmful organic materials. First, place the coral into a plastic bucket with an 8 percent solution of household bleach and soak it, preferably with an air stone operating, for one week. Then soak the coral in freshwater, to which has been added a commercial dechlorinator (liquid form, available at pet stores), for one day. After this, rinse the coral well and allow it to dry in the sun. Check for chlorine odor before installing the coral in your aquarium.

Coral replicas, cast from molds of real coral, are an ecologically responsible alternative to coral skeletons. They are nearly indistinguishable from the real thing, especially when exhibited in an aquarium with live green algae, and are constructed of nontoxic materials.

Living plants are important for the overall health of marine aquariums. They will allow you to achieve decorative effects not possible in an entirely artificial system. The well-planted habitat will allow for the establishment of territories and provide natural holdfasts for your pets.

Seaweed quickly comes to mind when one thinks of marine plants. The organisms erroneously referred to as seaweed are, in actuality, marine algae or, more specifically, macromarine

as lace rock and lava rock, are safe and commercially available. Coral rock will help maintain a safe pH level.

Live rock refers to rocks with their encrusting colonies of marine tube worms, sponges, algae. Macroalgae are distinguished from true plants by the absence of roots, stems, and leaves. (They have, however, the ecological equivalents of these structures.) Macroalgae may be single celled or multicelled. A true plant adapted to the marine environment is eelgrass, which is not easily established in the aquarium.

The hardiest of the macroalgae is *Caulerpa prolifera*. It is also one of the best species to use with seahorses because its blades are long, narrow, and much like the sea grass favored by so many species. Seahorses readily swim between the blades and anchor upon them. The blade arrangement provides a great deal of cover in a small area, thus increasing the carrying capacity by allowing for privacy and physical barriers. This alga spreads by sending out runners, or rhizomes, that attach to the substrate. It reproduces rapidly. Commercially available trace elements should be added where heavy growths are established. Although native to Florida and more southerly waters, this alga is cultivated commercially in Europe. The closely related *Caulerpa asheadii*, also native to Florida, grows in a similar manner and does well in the aquarium.

Calcareous algae use calcium to produce fairly rigid blades. Heavy growths will require the addition of calcium and other trace elements to the water. The shaving brush, *Penicillus capitatus*, is slow growing but hardy. It produces thin filaments that make excellent anchorage sites for small seahorses.

TIP

In addition to trace elements, green algae requires light of a sufficient intensity and duration.

Sea cactus, *Udotea flabellum*, is a calcareous alga that does well in warm-water aquariums. It is suitable for use with larger seahorse species.

A variety of plastic marine algae replicas are available for use in saltwater aquariums. A good technique is to purchase plastic replicas of species that are unavailable commercially or are difficult to propagate. When interspersed among a growth of live algae, you can create a very realistic impression. Be sure that the plants you purchase are specifically designed for use in saltwater aquariums—those with internal metal supports will quickly poison the water.

Microalgae will likely develop on most surfaces within the aquarium. Those species that are green in color are desirable as oxygen producers. They also help to remove nitrates from the water. They require more light than do the brown and red algae and usually arrive as cells attached to an animal or in its water. Green algae can also be seeded with the scrapings from an established aquarium. A coating of green algae also improves the appearance of artificial plants and rocks.

CONDITIONING AND CARING FOR YOUR AQUARIUM

The newly set up, crystal clear aquarium is, unfortunately, not yet ready to house seahorses. A series of important and, for seahorses, traumatic chemical changes known as the nitrogen cycle have yet to occur. Seahorses are, in general, too sensitive to survive this initial conditioning period.

The nitrogen cycle is the process where nitrogen in food, excretory products, and dead organisms are converted to other organic compounds that are then used by plants and animals. Ammonia is the most toxic nitrogen compound to seahorses and other marine creatures. In the aquarium, it accumulates as a by-product of the decay of uneaten food and dead organisms. It is also excreted by the tank's inhabitants. The term *total ammonia* refers to the level of two chemical forms of the compound, ionized ammonia and un-ionized ammonia. Ammonia in its un-ionized form is most toxic to marine organisms. The proportion of the total ammonia in the un-ionized form increases as the pH and temperature rise.

Careful attention to detail will result in crystal-clear aquarium water (thorny seahorse, H. hystrix).

Bacteria and the Nitrogen Cycle

The next phase of the nitrogen cycle, termed nitrification, is controlled by the actions of two species of aerobic bacteria. Aerobic bacteria require oxygen to survive. They develop huge populations on substrates through which oxygenated water is circulated, such as gravel beds above undergravel filters and the filter materials in outside filters. Bacteria of the genus *Nitrosomonas* convert ammonia into less toxic (but still dangerous) compounds known as nitrites. *Nitrobacter* sp. bacteria metabolize the nitrites and, in doing so, convert them to the least toxic of the nitrogenous compounds, nitrates.

Until large populations of these bacteria are established, the ammonia, nitrate, and nitrite levels will be toxic to seahorses. This conditioning period generally takes from four to six weeks. However, each aquarium is unique in this respect. Some fish are, however, required during this period in order to provide the waste products upon which the beneficial bacteria feed. Several hardy species are ideal for this purpose. The domino damselfish is used most commonly. Four or five specimens in a 55-gallon (200-L) tank should suffice. You could also use a striped killifish (*Fundulud majalis*). Be sure to arrange for homes for these fish once the conditioning period is complete. Both species are aggressive feeders and will consume all food before the seahorses have a chance to feed.

Adding bacteria: The length of the conditioning period can be shortened by adding commercially available live bacteria. Both the freeze-dried and liquid forms work well. Another option is to introduce gravel from a healthy, well-established aquarium. Filter material from such a tank can also be added to your outside filter. (When changing your own filter, retain a bit of the old material for seeding purposes.) Neither of these options eliminates the need for a conditioning period. However, they can shorten its length.

Monitoring the nitrogen cycle: During the first part of the conditioning period, you will need to test ammonia levels daily. Commercial kits are available. Ammonia levels will rise

rapidly because the bacteria numbers are low. Ammonia levels generally peak in one to two weeks and then drop off rapidly as the bacteria multiply. At this point, nitrites will appear as a by-product of *Nitrosomonas* bacteria metabolism. Daily checks of nitrite levels will reveal a pattern similar to that described for ammonia, this time under the control of the *Nitrobacter* sp. bacteria. Nitrite levels will suddenly drop off as the bacteria increase, signifying an end to the conditioning period.

You should routinely perform a pH test during this period because the pH will likely drop at some point. A pH level of less than 8.0 will retard the actions of the nitrifying bacteria. Seahorses fare well at a pH level of 8.0 to 8.3.

Aquarium Chemistry

The salinity of water is more properly termed its specific gravity or density. A specific gravity reading expresses the ratio of total dissolved salts in water. The standard of comparison is pure water, which has a specific gravity of 1.000. Many salts contribute to the reading, among them sodium chloride (table salt) and magnesium chloride.

A hydrometer is used to measure specific gravity. Two main types are marketed for use with home aquariums. The original version is a glass tube that rises higher in the water as specific gravity increases. The scale is read at the waterline. Perfectly still water is required for an accurate reading. The density of water decreases due to expansion as temperature rises, so hydrometers are standardized at a particular temperature. A conversion table is used when the water is at nonstandard temperatures. A newer hydrometer, consisting of a

---

TIP

Very high levels of ammonia and nitrites should be managed with partial water changes.

A hydrometer in use.

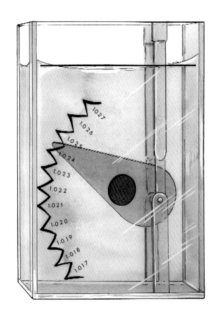

plastic case with an internal scale, is easier to use and requires no standardization.

You should take specific gravity readings regularly. Salts do not evaporate along with water, so specific gravity increases as water evaporates. Declines in specific gravity, which are less common, can be corrected by adding synthetic marine salts.

In general, a specific gravity reading of 1.020 to 1.023 will meet the needs of most seahorses. You should research the exact requirement of the species you are interested in, however. The few species that inhabit estuaries may be adapted to a lower-than-usual specific gravity or may require fluctuating levels if they are to thrive.

Oxygen: Marine environments generally have high levels of dissolved oxygen. This situation should be duplicated in the aquarium. Oxygen exchange occurs at the aquarium's surface. Water movement caused by the filter outflow or bubbling of air stones increases the surface area for oxygen transfer. Note that the oxygen in the bubbles escapes into the air and does not add to the water's dissolved oxygen content. Remember that many seahorse species are adapted to quiet waters. For these animals, the currents caused by strong filtration would likely lead to stress, poor feeding success, and a short life span. Aeration provided by air stones is generally an effective way to increase the aquarium's dissolved oxygen content. Alternatively, many new filters are equipped with devices to control water outflow.

The beneficial bacteria in the aquarium (see page 25) require a flow of oxygenated water to thrive. Those in the filter bed, gravel bed, and filter materials are supplied with oxygen-rich water circulated by the motor operating these devices.

As the temperature of water rises, its ability to hold dissolved oxygen decreases. This can be a problem in the summertime, even if the temperature itself is suitable for seahorses. Seahorse species inhabiting cool, open waters will likely have higher oxygen requirements than species native to sheltered, tropical habitats.

Temperature: Seahorses are, in general, creatures adapted to areas of fairly stable temperatures. Tropical species, in particular, may experience little change in temperature throughout the year. Those types that inhabit areas exposed to seasonal change generally move offshore during the cooler months and thus are not exposed to frequent temperature changes. The aquarist must remember that seahorses, like the vast majority of fish, are ectothermic (cold-blooded). As such, they are unable to regulate their body temperatures without moving to a warmer or cooler location. In the wild, seahorses can migrate from areas of unsuitable temperature. However, in the aquarium, they are at the mercy of their keeper.

Temperature change can be an important stimulant to breeding. Any such changes should be made gradually. Ideally, they should be in accordance with the seasonal changes that occur in the seahorse's natural habitat. Although sudden temperature changes can stimulate breeding in many amphibians and invertebrates, whether such is the case with seahorses is not known. As with most fish, sudden temperature changes often lead to shock in seahorses or infestation by opportunistic parasites. The thermostats of most aquarium heaters allow for the fine tuning necessary to avoid sudden temperature changes. For temperature-sensitive species being kept in cold climates, installing a second heater and setting the thermostat at the lowest safe temperature is wise. Having a second heater is important because heaters give no indication of imminent failure. You therefore will need to

have a backup heater set to come on when the temperature dips.

Bear in mind that warm water holds less oxygen than does cool water. Also, the metabolic rate of your seahorses will increase with rising temperature, resulting in a need for higher oxygen levels. Increased aeration and spacious enclosures are therefore prudent during warm times.

pH is the measure of the water's acidity or alkalinity. A reading of 7 is considered neutral. A reading of 1 is the most acidic point, and 14 is the point of greatest alkalinity. Natural seawater has a pH of 8 or slightly above. The aquarium should have a similar pH; 8.3 is a safe upper limit for seahorses.

Acidity and alkalinity in both natural and artificial systems are affected by a variety of chemical processes. The pH tends to drift downward (become acidic) when acids are released during the nitrogen cycle and during the respiration of animals (carbon dioxide becomes carbonic acid). In the ocean, the acidification process is retarded by buffers, such as bicarbonate and carbonates. The pH in most marine systems is thus very stable. In the aquarium, rapid pH changes are common, especially when fish wastes and uneaten food have built up. These changes can be fatal to the tank's inhabitants. Effective bacterial filtration and adequate aeration will help avoid some of the downward drift in pH. Equally important is the choice of substrate. Crushed coral and shell, limestone, dolomite, and coral are effective buffering agents that will help maintain appropriate pH levels. These materials lose their buffering capacity over time, however. Therefore, conducting routine (at least weekly) pH tests with a commercially available kit is

An example of a common pH testing kit.

extremely important. Simple kits, which utilize a color comparison chart, are sufficient for use with aquariums containing seahorses.

Natural seawater: To many people, *seawater* is synonymous with *salt water*. While sodium chloride (table salt) is its most abundant compound, natural seawater is actually an extremely complex liquid. A huge array of chemicals, organic and inorganic compounds, and elements give seawater its unique characteristics. Calcium carbonate, magnesium chloride, and magnesium sulfate are among seawater's most abundant inorganic compounds, while elements present in seawater include selenium, molybdenum, and zinc. Microorganisms such as phytoplankton and zooplankton, as well as suspended organic materials, give seawater from different locations unique characteristics.

Natural seawater is an excellent medium in which to keep seahorses and is used by many of the world's most successful public aquariums. However, you should consider several important points before deciding upon this route. First, for all its stability in the natural state, seawater undergoes rapid chemical changes in the aquarium. Trace elements must be replenished from time to time. This can be accomplished by regular water changes with natural seawater or by using commercially available mixtures. Also, most samples will contain huge populations of planktonic organisms, which will generally not survive confinement. Their death and decomposition will increase ammonia levels and cause other chemical changes that are harmful to seahorses and other organisms.

You should also consider the possibility that the seawater will introduce disease or parasites, such as fish lice, into the aquarium. Pollutants such as lawn and garden chemicals, sewage, and chemical wastes are also a real concern. This is especially true in inshore areas and in shallow areas with limited water exchange, such as bays and lagoons. Pollution may also be of concern in the open sea. In most instances, you are wiser to collect seawater from as far offshore as is practical and safe. Water from ocean beaches will, in all likelihood, be of better quality than that from enclosed bays.

Water should be collected in a plastic container that has not previously held harmful chemicals (these may leach into the plastic and be difficult to rinse out). Springwater containers are ideal. After collection, the water should be stored in a sealed container in a dark area for at least one week. This will allow the phytoplankton and zooplankton to die off. Their bodies and other suspended particles will form a sediment at the bottom of the container, which you should discard before using the water.

You should test the temperature, pH, ammonia, nitrate, and nitrite levels of the water, and make the appropriate adjustments. Allow the water to filter for at least 24 hours before using it.

Artificial seawater: Commercially available synthetic sea salt mixes provide a suitable alternative to natural seawater. Reputable brands are well balanced and often include trace elements. Replace these as directed by the manufacturer. Most mix readily with water. Using them eliminates several concerns associated with the use of natural seawater (plankton populations, pollution, long-term storage, and so on). Remember that the water used to mix your artificial seawater must be treated with a chemical preparation to remove chloramine and chloride. Such preparations are available at pet stores and work instantly. If using tap or well water, you should check the nitrate and phosphate levels, as high levels of either will cause algae blooms. If your tap water is unsuitable, a reverse osmosis (RO) unit might be a worthwhile purchase.

Equipment

Lighting: In addition to allowing you to view your aquarium's inhabitants, proper lighting is necessary to maintain seahorse health. It encourages normal activity patterns and the establishment of living marine algae.

The most commonly kept seahorse species are creatures of shallow, brightly lit waters. You should duplicate these conditions in captivity, providing darker, secluded areas for use as retreats. Changes in photoperiod (the length of daylight) encourage breeding in many species of fish and may do so for seahorses also, especially those from temperate regions. Ideally, you should duplicate the photoperiod of your seahorses' natural habitat. This can be easily accomplished with a light timer. If you employ more than one light fixture, you can arrange the timers to allow a period of gradually increasing daylight in the morning and gradually increasing darkness in the evening. This system will give you the best opportunity to observe natural behavior and the best chance of breeding success. Nightlights, which produce light of a wavelength invisible to fish, will allow you to peek into the little-known world of the nighttime behavior of seahorses.

A variety of fluorescent bulbs is available for lighting your aquarium. Those specifically designed to stimulate plant growth will emit a greater amount of light in the red and blue wavelengths. These also tend to enhance the colors of seahorses and of other marine organisms. Broad or full-spectrum bulbs are designed to mimic sunlight and will also enhance the appearance of the colors of your pets. Bulbs specifically designed for use with plants will also allow a healthy growth of green algae to develop. These will help manage carbon dioxide levels and will also provide food for a wide variety of seahorse-compatible invertebrates.

Light in the red and blue wavelengths may encourage the growth of undesirable species of brown algae, however. Most types of marine algae will require a photoperiod of 10 to 14 hours per day and a light source of greater intensity than that required by simple algae. Remember that intensity refers to the output of the bulb. This measurement is independent of wattage. The light intensity required will also be affected by the depth of your aquarium. Marine fish dealers and bulb manufacturers can counsel you in the selection of appropriate bulbs. High-output lamps and metal halide bulbs are available. However, they are generally unnecessary for all but the very largest aquariums. Metal halide lamps emit a great deal of heat and must be used in conjunction with a fan or chiller.

Heat: A careful study of your seahorses' natural history and range will provide you with guidelines about their temperature requirements. Beware of making broad judgments concerning temperature based on ranges. Sheltered inlets, for example, may be considerably warmer or cooler than the

*There are a number of thermometer
types from which to choose.*

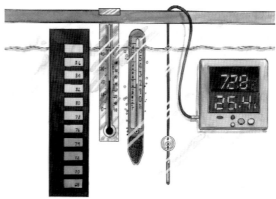

nearby ocean, and oceanic currents can
result in very cold water temperatures even
in tropical areas. Tropical species will thrive,
in general, at temperatures ranging from
76°F to 83°F (24.5°C to 28.3°C). Gravid
females and brooding males may require
warmer temperatures.

Temperature can be easily manipulated to
encourage breeding. Temperate species may
benefit from a cool period during the winter.
Many temperate invertebrates, fish, amphibians, and reptiles will not successfully reproduce
without a dormancy period. This may well be
true for certain seahorse species. Little is known
about this topic as it relates to seahorses, and
the area is ripe for investigation by enterprising
hobbyists. Likewise, temperature spikes stimulate courtship in some animals. In general, however, temperature stability will be the rule
because sudden changes bring on illness.

The heater you need will depend on the size
of your aquarium and the temperature of the
room in which the aquarium is kept. For rooms
that stay at 68°F (20°C) or higher, 2 watts per
gallon (per 3.8 L) is sufficient. For cooler locations, you need 5 watts per gallon (per 3.8 L).
Older heater models must be mounted via suc-
tion cups so that the control knob or dial is
above the waterline. Newer types are completely submersible and are easier to hide or
disguise. Choose a model that has a thermostat
that allows you to choose a specific temperature as opposed to one that is calibrated with
only broad categories such as high and low.
Follow the manufacturer's instructions for
installation. Do not position the heater near

the filter outflow because the constant rush
of water may disturb the sensors and distort
the reading. Also, always leave your heater
unplugged for 20 minutes or so before
removing it from the aquarium or if you are
doing a water change that will drop the water
level and expose the heater. If the heater has
been running and is hot, its glass container will
crack upon contact with the air. You must
monitor the heater carefully until the desired
temperature is reached. A red light will indicate
that the heater is on. The heater (and the light)
will switch off when the temperature set on
the thermostat is established. Turning the dial
a bit lower will hold the temperature at that
point. Broad-range thermostats (high/low ones)
are more difficult to set and require closer
attention during operation.

You should install a second heater as a
backup because your main heater will not give
warning of imminent failure. The backup
heater should be set at the lowest temperature
that is appropriate for your seahorses, so that
it will come on only if the main heater fails to
operate.

Use an all-glass thermometer. Do not use a thermometer that contains metal. It will rust and poison the seahorses. Situate the thermometer across the aquarium from the heater. This will allow you to judge the accuracy of your thermometer to a better degree than if the thermometer were placed near the heater. Alcohol-filled thermometers are safer than those containing mercury, which will poison your seahorses if the thermometer is accidentally broken. Plastic strip thermometers that stick to the outside of the aquarium are also available. They are filled with temperature-sensitive crystals and are only slightly less accurate than the traditional models. The stick-on models should also be placed far from the heater. Periodically using an in-tank thermometer will check the accuracy.

Filtration refers to the natural and artificial processes and the mechanical equipment used to maintain water quality in the aquarium. A thorough understanding of the nitrogen cycle is essential for setting up and maintaining an appropriate filtration system. Simply, the nitrogen cycle is a natural process in which aerobic (oxygen-using) bacteria use nitrogen-based compounds (which are toxic to most marine organisms) for energy. In the process, they transform the nitrogen compounds into less harmful substances. Specifically, various nitrogenous bacteria transform, through their metabolism, the ammonia present in animal waste and uneaten food into nitrite, which is less toxic. The nitrite is then metabolized by other bacteria and transformed into nitrate, the least toxic of the nitrogen-based compounds. Denitrifying bacteria then convert the nitrate to free nitrogen and nitrous oxide. For a more detailed explanation of the nitrogen cycle and its importance to marine aquarium maintenance, see page 25.

The functioning of the nitrogen cycle is greatly altered within the confines of an aquarium. Human intervention is necessary to prevent the gradual poisoning of the aquarium's inhabitants due to the buildup of toxic waste products. Three basic types of filtration can be used—biological, chemical, and mechanical. Although each has a specific purpose, they overlap with one another to some extent.

Biological filtration concerns the detoxification of nitrogen-based compounds by using the nitrogen cycle. Significant biological filtration effects can be achieved with fluidized bed, trickle, and mechanical filters and by adding live rocks to the aquarium.

Chemical filtration removes dissolved organic compounds from aquarium water. These compounds arise as a by-product of animal metabolism and are also present in uneaten food and dead organisms. A high concentration of dissolved organic material is manifested by a yellowish tint to the water. Filtration and water changes should be used to prevent dissolved organic materials from reaching the level where they are visibly coloring the water, because they are harmful to marine life.

The actual filtration is performed by a variety of substances and, in some cases, by specially treated filter pads. These materials and pads can be added to a wide variety of filters. Canister filters, outside filters, and box filters can all accommodate chemical filtration media. Small canisters that attach to undergravel airlift return tubes can also be filled with chemical filtration materials, but the amount that can be utilized is very small. Protein skimmers

Live rock helps maintain water quality and provides anchorage sites.

and ultraviolet sterilizers are also used to carry out chemical filtration.

Activated carbon is the most commonly used chemical filtration medium. The solid form is most effective for aquarium use. Filter pads impregnated with activated carbon are useful as supplementary filter materials. Ammonia-removing substances are also widely available and should be used in conjunction with activated carbon in all aquariums.

In mechanical filtration, suspended particles are trapped as water moves through material such as foam pads, filter floss, gravel, or sand. Outside filters and canister filters function well as mechanical filters. Significant mechanical filtration is also achieved with undergravel filters. In this case, the particulate matter is trapped within the gravel bed. Regular removal of this material with a siphon-based gravel washer is therefore essential. Reverse-flow undergravel filters result in less accumulation of waste products within the gravel bed. However, the material is recirculated into the water column, and therefore a supplementary mechanical filter is required.

Live rock: The term *live rock* refers to rocks that are taken from the ocean, complete with their encrusting flora and fauna, and are established in the aquarium. The innumerable organisms coating even a small piece of such rock can include bacteria, protozoa, microcrustaceans, sponges, mollusks, algae, and other life-forms. The role these organisms play in the ecology of the aquarium is not completely understood. It is known, however, that the ever-present nitrifying bacteria assist in biological filtration by converting ammonia to less toxic compounds such as nitrites and nitrates. In fact, if you pay careful attention to the number of organisms maintained in the aquarium, marine aquariums may be kept with live rock as their sole form of filtration. Such an undertaking requires a thorough understanding of marine ecology, water chemistry, and the animals that are maintained. Only experienced aquarists should attempt this.

The organisms coating live rock also use food missed by other aquarium inhabitants and the actual waste products of the larger animals. Certain species may even reproduce in the aquarium, thereby providing tiny food items for even the smallest seahorse fry. If you decide to include live rock in your aquarium, please be sure that you purchase only farmed rocks and do not collect them from the wild or buy from unknown sources. Be aware that some of the organisms colonizing the rocks may die when introduced into the aquarium. You should carefully monitor ammonia levels after introducing live rock.

Water Changes

Regular water changes are vital adjuncts to all filtration systems regardless of how effective the filtration is or how carefully the system is maintained. In most instances, a 25 percent change each month is sufficient. This figure will, however, vary greatly depending upon the situation. For example, more frequent changes and changes of greater volume may be required during the break-in period when the aquarium is first established or where large numbers of seahorses are maintained. Regardless of filtration, if regular water changes are not performed, the levels of harmful nitrogenous compounds will increase, and the water's pH, buffering capacity, and trace-element content will decrease.

The replacement water should ideally be prepared beforehand and allowed to circulate overnight. The water used to mix your replacement seawater should be treated with a chemical to remove chlorine and chloramine. It should also be of approximately the same temperature as the water in your aquarium. Be sure to add the new water slowly or allow it to overflow from a clean glass vessel to avoid disturbing the substrate and your seahorses.

Water lost during evaporation should be replaced with dechlorinated water and not seawater. This is because the salts present in seawater cannot evaporate but remain within the aquarium. As the water level drops, they become more concentrated and the specific gravity increases. Adding seawater

Live rock functions as ornamentation, an anchorage site, and additional filtration.

Changing the water using a gravel cleaner.

to make up for water lost through evaporation will cause the specific gravity (salinity) to rise even higher and will eventually kill your seahorses.

Types of Filters

An undergravel filter consists of a perforated plastic plate set onto the bottom of the aquarium. Gravel or another form of substrate is placed on top of this plate, which acts as a false bottom and creates an area below through which water can circulate. The substrate must be large enough not to slip through the perforations in the undergravel plate. The substrate bed should be at least 3 inches (7.5 cm) in depth but can be greater. Plastic tubes connected to each end of the plate allow for connection to the air pump or power head that operates the filter. The pump or power head pulls water through the gravel bed and up the plastic tubes. Water exiting the airlift tubes provides aeration for the aquarium's inhabitants. At one time, undergravel filters were standard aquarium equipment, but today they have been largely replaced by fluidized bed filters.

The flow of oxygenated water through the gravel bed allows aerobic (oxygen-using) bacteria to become established. These bacteria perform biological filtration, metabolizing ammonia and nitrites into the less harmful nitrates. The substrate itself provides a large surface area upon which the bacteria can grow. Without the flow of oxygenated water through the gravel bed, harmful aerobic bacteria develop. These bacteria release methane gas,

TIP

The most effective method of removing water from the aquarium is to use a siphon fitted with a gravel cleaner. This implement will remove detritus from the substrate bed along with the water.

which is detrimental to seahorses and other marine fish.

Mechanical filtration also occurs with undergravel filters as suspended particulate matter becomes trapped in the gravel or substrate bed. This material must be periodically removed with a siphon-based gravel washer. You should also remove the outflow tubes and insert the siphon below the filter plate when removing the suspended particulates. Doing so will allow you to dispose of the sludge that can accumulate there.

Power heads greatly increase the flow of water through the substrate. However, the resulting current leaving the filter's outflow tubes may be too strong for most seahorse species. Newer models are adjustable, so you can maintain a more appropriate flow. Another alternative is to set the power head to its reverse-flow mode. This will result in water being pulled down the airlift tube and circulated up through the gravel bed. (In standard-

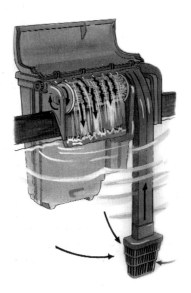

flow mode, water is pulled into the gravel bed and then exits the airlift.) Using the reverse-flow system creates very little surface disturbance or water currents. Depending on your aquarium's size and the number of animals maintained, mild supplementary aeration may be necessary. Also, less particulate matter is retained in the substrate bed when this mode of operation is used. Therefore, supplemental mechanical filtration is required to remove suspended materials from the water.

Undergravel filters were once a standard piece of marine aquarium equipment. They have fallen out of favor, though, and are now rarely used by public aquariums. Their main asset is that they do not remove small food items from the aquarium. However, biological filtration is more effectively carried out by fluidized bed filters. A major drawback of undergravel filters is that during a power outage, the aerobic bacteria in the aquarium will die off. Consequently, poisonous methane gas will be quickly produced by opportunistic anaerobic bacteria.

Outside filters may be boxes that hang on the back of the aquarium or canister types that sit on the floor below the aquarium. Both employ a self-contained motor to draw water through a series of filter mediums. Mechanical filtration (particulate removal) is performed by the filter floss, filter pads, or cartridges. Chemical filtration is carried out by activated carbon, ammonia removers, and other materials. Biological filtration also occurs because the circulation of oxygenated water allows for the development of nitrogenous bacteria on the filter pads, floss, activated carbon, and other materials used in the filter. The surface area

An outside filter.

available to the bacteria, however, is much smaller than that provided by the substrate bed. Therefore, the biological aspect is not as efficient as that provided by an undergravel filter. The return of clean water to the aquarium disturbs the surface and provides aeration for the seahorses. Large filters can produce strong return currents, so be sure that a defuser is attached. Otherwise, your seahorses may have difficulty swimming, catching food, and behaving normally. If you use an older model, a defuser may not be available. In this case plants, corals, or other aquarium furniture may be positioned in front of the outflow to divert and slow down the return currents.

Follow the manufacturer's recommendations concerning the amount of various filter materials to use. You will need to replace these periodically depending on the number of seahorses in your aquarium, the material used, and the type of filter. When replacing filtration materials, retain a bit of used carbon and filter floss. Add this along with the new materials to the clean filter. This will seed the beneficial bacteria into the filter and allow for a continuation of biological filtration (in most circumstances, the bacteria reproduce rapidly under favorable conditions). Always rinse new filter materials well because activated carbon, in particular, contains dust that may cloud your water. The inside of your filter box (the area that holds the filtration material) should be cleaned with temperate water only and not hot water. The interior of the box will also be coated with beneficial bacteria, and hot water will kill them. You do not need to scrub the inside of the box—a mere rinse will do. The same applies to reusable filter pads. Clean them with temperate water only.

Wet/dry filters: Although originally designed for complex coral reef aquariums and public exhibits, scaled-down models of wet/dry filters are now marketed for use in home marine aquariums. These are sometimes known as trickle or nitrifying/denitrifying filters. A prefilter removes large detritus. The biological filtration medium (gravel or plastic bio balls) is not submerged as in traditional filters but, rather, is moistened by a constant drip or spray of water from the aquarium. This encourages the growth of huge populations of aerobic nitrifying bacteria and results in very effective biological filtration. A separate chamber houses anaerobic bacteria, which assists in the denitrification (the conversion of nitrate to nitrous oxide and free nitrogen). Unless you are housing your seahorses with corals, sponges, or other delicate, filter-feeding invertebrates, you do not need to invest in this complex and often expensive filtration system.

Fluidized bed filters are often used by public aquariums. These filtration devices are now readily available to hobbyists. The filter consists of a plastic, sand-filled tube through which water is circulated. All of the sand is kept in constant motion, providing an enormous surface area for the growth of aerobic bacteria. This therefore achieves exceptional biological filtration. Fluidized bed filters should be installed in all marine aquariums. Using these filters avoids the problem of detritus lodged in the aquarium substrate, which occurs when using undergravel filters. Only a thin layer of gravel is needed, and this gravel is easily cleared.

Protein skimmers: The main function of protein skimmers (foam fractionators) is to remove dissolved organic compounds such as proteins and peptides from aquarium water by a process known as desaturation. They function by combining air bubbles with organic material and carrying them, as foam, to a separate collection area. The foam liquifies in this chamber and is periodically discarded. Protein skimmers also remove important trace elements from the water, so you must add these elements regularly. Protein skimmers are not absolutely necessary for seahorse maintenance (unless you keep them with delicate marine invertebrates such as corals). However, you should consider using them.

Ozone generators use energized oxygen molecules to break down organic compounds and to kill various microorganisms. Ozone is also highly toxic to fish, so great care must be used. Ozone generators are not required for seahorse maintenance, but additional research may lead to their use in the treatment of fish diseases.

Ultraviolet sterilizers irradiate water with ultraviolet light to kill fungi, bacteria, and other potentially harmful microorganisms. Their use in the past has been limited to large public aquariums, but small models are now readily available. They may have an application in disease treatment, but their use with seahorses is as yet unexplored.

Box filters are situated within the aquarium and are powered by an air pump. As with outside and canister filters, water is circulated through filter floss in the mechanical filtration phase of operation. Chemical filtration is carried out by activated carbon, ammonia removers, and other mediums. Biological filtration occurs when beneficial nitrifying bacteria become established on the filtration materials within the filter. The small size of most box filters limits their use, however. They also detract from the aquarium's appearance unless well hidden. Their main application is in quarantine aquariums and in raising seahorse fry. They are especially useful in raising fry because the air flow to them can be controlled with gang valves. There is thus little likelihood of the weakly swimming young seahorses being drawn into the filter. Another useful aspect of box filters is that the water outflow is directed upward, thereby reducing currents that may disturb seahorses. Maintenance of the filtration material is the same as for outside filters (see page 36).

A sponge filter is basically a porous sponge connected to an air pump to perform chemical and biological filtration. A sponge filter is placed inside the aquarium. The sponge's porous surface allows for the growth of large populations of aerobic, nitrifying bacteria. It also retains particulate matter as water passes through. The sponge is removed periodically and cleaned by rinsing with temperate water. As with other replaceable filter materials, do not rinse it with hot water. Doing so will kill the useful bacteria growing within. A sponge filter is especially useful when raising seahorse fry, because no danger exists of drawing the tiny animals into the filter media. It can also be set with a weak enough current so that even brine

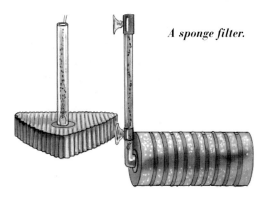

A sponge filter.

shrimps will be left unharmed. Outflow is directed upward, so currents are minimal.

Chemical filtration is not possible unless a separate cartridge is attached to the airlift tube. Such cartridges are usually small and contain a bit of activated carbon. The filtration they perform is minimal, so frequent water changes are the rule when using sponge filters. Some models have attached, submersible motors and use carbon-impregnated pads. These create strong return-flow currents but are otherwise similar in form and function to a traditional sponge filter.

Cleaning and Maintenance

Paying careful attention when establishing your aquarium and installing the filtration system will lessen the routine maintenance. However, you should never ignore routine maintenance. Doing so is tempting, especially when the water is crystal clear and the seahorses appear in vibrant good health. Water quality can, however, deteriorate rapidly. In some instances, you may not be given warning signs before your fish expire.

The routine maintenance schedules set out below will insure that you remain abreast of potential problems. Please be aware that salt water is an excellent conductor of electricity. All electric appliances, including lights, must be disconnected before they are serviced.

You should purchase several plastic 5-gallon (20-L) buckets to use during aquarium maintenance and set them aside for this purpose only. Most plastics are quite porous and will retain harmful chemicals. The only disinfectant that you will likely need is bleach. Items cleaned with bleach must be soaked and rinsed as described on page 22 before being returned to the aquarium. Be particularly careful to remove all traces of soap and other chemicals from your hands before placing them into the aquarium.

Daily Maintenance

A visual inspection of the animals is the first and most basic duty to perform each day. A particularly good time to do this is during feeding, although you should also check while the animals are anchored to holdfasts. As seahorses are not overly active creatures, signs of illness will be less apparent than they are for other types of fish. Also, clamped fins, a universal sign of poor condition in fish, are less evident on seahorses because of their physical makeup. You must therefore be intimately familiar with your seahorses' normal behavior, swimming position, and feeding routine. While observing your seahorses, be sure that all are feeding and that dominant individuals are not monopolizing a majority of the food. You must also be very careful to check the condition of any sessile invertebrates (sponges and sea cucumbers) that you may house with your seahorses. Illness and death in such animals are easy to miss. The decaying corpses of such animals can quickly poison your water. Perform an ammonia test immediately if you find a dead organism.

Keep a fine mesh net handy (brine shrimp nets are ideal) to remove any visible debris or dead plant material each morning. You should also check all the electric equipment, such as filters, heaters, and lights. Decreased water flow may mean that the filter medium is dirty or that the gravel bed is becoming clogged with retained debris. It may also indicate a motor malfunction. Backups of each piece of electric equipment should be on hand. Accumulated salts in air lines or on air stones will interfere with air and water flow, so be sure to check for this as well.

Always check that your backup heater has not come on. Operation of the backup heater will indicate a possible low temperature and malfunction of your main heater. If the temperature has dipped below normal, be sure to make all temperature adjustments gradually and to check the water temperature after each adjustment is made to the heater.

While a completely malfunctioning lightbulb will be obvious, be aware that the intensity of your fluorescent bulb will gradually decrease over time. This will negatively affect the growth of marine algae in your aquarium. An easy way to avoid this is to note the end of the effective life of the bulb on a calendar or in another convenient spot. The manufacturer provides information about the effective life, which is generally given in hours. Therefore, you will need to compute the bulb's useful life based on its daily duration of operation.

While water quality tests will keep track of gradual changes in the water chemistry, immediately investigate any sudden change in appearance such as cloudiness or a foul odor. Usually the source is a dead organism or a filter malfunction.

TIP

Safety First and Always
Never leave razor blades on the floor—especially if you have children or pets.

Weekly Maintenance

Check the aquarium's water level weekly. Maintaining a constant water level is important because evaporation will concentrate salts in the water and raise the overall salinity (salts do not evaporate). A decrease in water volume will also concentrate harmful waste products that will then be all the more dangerous to the aquarium's inhabitants. The replacement water should be of approximately the same temperature as the aquarium water. Ideally, it should be mixed beforehand and circulated for a day or so before use. Be sure to treat the replacement water to remove chlorine and chloramine.

You should remove accumulated salt from all aquarium surfaces and equipment with a damp cloth. If you observe overly heavy salt buildup, be sure to check your specific gravity so that the loss of salt does not cause a potentially harmful change in specific gravity.

Clean glass makes an amazing difference in the appearance of the aquarium and in your ability to observe the subtle aspects of seahorse behavior. Outside aquarium glass may be cleaned with a commercial glass cleaner if you are careful not to spray any into the water. A razor blade or a nonabrasive algae sponge is best for cleaning the interior surfaces. (Note: Do not use razor blades on acrylic aquariums.) Be sure that any pad used is specifically designed for use on aquarium glass or acrylic so as not to cause scratches. Special pads are available for acrylic aquariums. Razor blades and algae pads may be handheld or purchased with extendable handles. Be careful when cleaning near the substrate line, as rough materials rubbed against the glass will scratch it. Also be sure to clean the glass that protects the lightbulb from the aquarium water. This quickly becomes coated with salt, which will markedly cut down on the light reaching your aquarium and affect the appearance of the fish and the health of the living marine plants.

You should test several water quality parameters weekly. A test for pH is particularly important, as it always declines over time. Changes can be corrected with commercially available chemicals or a water change. Simple pH test kits that rely on a color comparison system are readily available and suitable for use with seahorses.

Specific gravity is tested with a hydrometer to determine the salinity. An increase in salinity is caused by evaporation of water and can be remedied by adding fresh, dechlorinated water. A low reading is generally caused by the condensation of salt on the aquarium hood and other implements. This occurs when water leaves the aquarium as a fine mist, driven by vigorous aeration or filter outflow. Making up a suitable amount of fresh seawater and adding that to the aquarium is easier than trying to determine the amount of marine salt mixture to add directly into the tank.

You should also check nitrate levels weekly and maintain them below 50 ppm. This will help keep tabs on the functioning of your filtration system.

Monthly Maintenance

As a general rule, you should replace filter substrate pads monthly. However, many factors,

---

TIP

Subtoxic levels of nitrate are detrimental to the health and the growth rate of some fish—especially seahorses.

---

like the number of fish kept and the type of filter used, will affect this time issue. Undergravel filters are cleaned by siphoning with a gravel washer, and should be used when you do monthly water changes (see page 34).

Nonliving aquarium decorations, such as coral skeletons and plastic coral, may be cleaned in bleach when necessary to remove particulate matter trapped within porous surfaces. (Note that a coating of green algae, however, is beneficial and imparts a natural appearance to unnatural objects within the aquarium). You must carefully rinse any items treated with bleach. For a detailed discussion of this procedure, see page 22.

Generally, you should test ammonia and nitrite levels only when the aquarium is first established or when a major change has occurred within the aquarium. Such a change might be a large increase in the tank's population, a significant die-off of organisms, or a change in the type of filtration used.

Rather than obscuring your view of your seahorses, a densely planted, well-thought-out aquarium will provide more interesting viewing than will a sterile environment. The author has found that the best way to exhibit animals is to allow them the option to behave normally and to remain out of sight when they so choose. Especially with small, shy creatures, a complex environment fosters a wide range of natural behaviors and often encourages courtship and breeding. When decorating your seahorse aquarium, remember that, with few exceptions (the dwarf seahorse, *Hippocampus zosterae*), mated pairs spend only a short time together each morning and then separate to forage independently. Plantings of macroalgae, or of plastic plants and strategically placed rocks and coral, will increase the usable area of your aquarium and, perhaps, increase its carrying capacity as well.

Substrate

The term *substrate* refers to the material that covers the bottom of the aquarium. Gravel and rocks marketed for freshwater aquariums are not suitable. Substrates used in marine aquariums must have a high buffering capacity to help maintain an appropriate pH level. You must use calcium-based materials. Suitable substrates include crushed coral, coral sand, oyster shell, crushed mixed shells, dolomite, or a combination of several of these.

Setting Up the Aquarium

You should set up your aquarium in its permanent location, as moving even a small water-filled tank can cause it to burst. Be sure that the site chosen is level and can support the aquarium's weight. Newly purchased aquariums should be filled with water and checked for leaks (rare, but it does happen). Aquariums that have previously held animals should be cleaned with a solution of 8 ounces (250 mL) of bleach per gallon (per 3.8 L) of water, then rinsed and refilled with freshwater. You should add a commercial dechlorination agent and allow the water to stand for 24 hours. After this time, rinse the aquarium again.

The substrate must be rinsed with freshwater. Even products labeled *rinsed* will

Coral, sand, and plastic plants are ideal components for a home aquarium.

contain dust and organic particles that may impart a long-lasting cloudiness to your water. The substrate should be rinsed in portions in a plastic bucket that has been purchased especially for this use (chemicals leach into plastic). Allow water to flow through the substrate (burying a hose within it works quite well) until the water runs clear. Please note that dolomite will continue to produce a cloudiness each time it is moved, even when clean.

The author mixes synthetic seawater outside of the aquarium so that adjustments are easier to make. Most commercially available salts readily dissolve, however, so mixing the water right within the aquarium is possible. Add water to the aquarium by pouring it first into a nontoxic container and allowing this to overflow into the tank. Doing this will avoid disturbing the substrate. Fill the tank approximately half full, and then add your plants, corals, and other furnishings. Once you are satisfied with your setup, fill the aquarium to the top, again taking care to avoid disturbing the substrate.

Plug in the pump and, by using the gang valves, adjust the airflow to each undergravel airlift tube. Be sure that your hands are dry before working with electric equipment as water in general and salt water in particular conducts electricity very efficiently. At this point, connect your additional equipment,

A completed aquarium set-up, ready for your new pet.

such as the outside filter, heater, and light. Make sure that each is working properly. Watch your temperature carefully for 24 hours until you become familiar with the workings of your heater's thermostat. You should also install a backup aquarium heater in case the main one malfunctions. Check the specific gravity after the water has been circulating for 24 hours so that any salts that may be trapped within the gravel bed have had a chance to dissolve. Testing too early will result in an artificially low reading.

NUTRITION AND FEEDING

The role of seahorse nutrition is of extreme importance and complexity, and a discussion of it touches upon nearly every other topic addressed in this book. The overlap in certain areas will be immediately apparent.

The Role of Nutrition

Consider the relationship between proper nutrition and good health. Also obvious, of course, is the fact that seahorses are extremely exacting in their food requirements. They are adapted to feed upon only living creatures of a certain size and nothing else. Less well-known is the quantity of food required. Adult seahorses consume 50 to 100 food items per day, while growing young may require over 3,000.

The influence of diet on other aspects of seahorse husbandry is less evident at first glance. Captive reproduction is particularly dependent on proper nutrition. Success in this area may necessitate short-term changes in the type and amount of food offered. The type of diet fed will also depend on such variables as the age of the aquarium's inhabitants and the temperature at which they are maintained. The complexity of these factors increases if a variety of seahorse species are housed together or

Nutrition is the least understood and most difficult aspect of seahorse husbandry.

if they are kept with animals such as pipefish or invertebrates.

The type of aquarium in which the seahorses live will also affect the way in which food is presented. Factors such as whether an uneaten food animal will live or die in the tank—for example, when freshwater animals are used as food—and how one will keep track of the food eaten by secretive aquarium inhabitants must all be considered.

Individual Food Items

The sections that follow will discuss individual food items. They will include feeding techniques and special considerations where appropriate. Unique nutritional situations, such as preparing adults for breeding, raising young, and managing the mixed-species aquarium, are included under separate headings elsewhere in the book.

Small, marine shrimps are among the most nutritious of foods for captive seahorses. Ideally, these should form the bulk of their diet.

Suitably sized individuals of the genera *Palaemonetes*, *Crago*, *Peneus*, and *Mysidopsis*—which are not actually true shrimps—can be collected along shorelines throughout the world. A seine dragged through eelgrass or other such cover will usually yield enormous numbers, as will a minnow trap baited with dead fish. An alternative method to collect them is to shake clumps of marine algae over a bucket.

Live shrimps are best transported in damp marine algae or in an aerated container of seawater. (In unaerated water, they tend to use up all of the oxygen and then die.) Many shrimps are quite hardy and will thrive in captivity. The shrimp-holding tank should be filtered and well lit in order to encourage the growth of algae. Provide ample hiding spots in the form of plastic or live plants, shells, and cracked crockery flowerpots. Tropical fish food flakes and algae tablets, those sold for such fish as *Plecostomus*, provide an adequate diet for most species. You should provide mysid, or opossum, shrimps, however, with live brine shrimps.

Shrimps are active, interesting creatures in their own right—so do not be surprised if you find yourself spending a good deal of time observing them. The females generally hold their eggs below their bodies until the eggs hatch. Plastic breeding grass—that sold for use with tropical fish—will make harvesting the young easier and will provide a refuge for the cannibalistic adults.

Mysid shrimps are not true shrimps but, rather, tiny crustaceans in their own order (Mysidacea). Although dubbed opossum shrimps because the female secretes her eggs into a brood pouch, they are quite shrimplike in behavior and appearance. Mysid shrimps

form the basis of captive seahorse diets in most public aquariums and are the most nutritionally complete food item available to hobbyists. They are quite easy to breed but require a supply of newly hatched brine shrimps as food. A 20-gallon (75-L) aquarium can house up to 125 breeding adults. Young should be siphoned out and established in a series of 5-gallon (20-L) or 10-gallon (40-L) tanks for rearing. The tanks should be equipped with sponge filters. The shrimp will mature at one month of age if kept at 75°F (23.6°C). At that time, a second, large breeding tank should be established, with a third to follow one month later. Feed the adults to your seahorses when you note a decline in egg production. Paying careful attention to the rotation of breeders and young will enable you to provide a constant food source for seahorses of all sizes.

Mysids are commercially available. You should establish a culture before you attempt to keep seahorses. If you do not have access to a year-round supply of wild shrimps, you will be unable to maintain any seahorse species for anything approaching a natural life span. The only exception is the dwarf seahorse (*Hippocampus zosterae*). The traditional diet of live brine shrimps will result in the early death of all except the dwarf seahorse.

Alternative sources of marine shrimps are bait shops, pet stores, and commercial shrimp farms. The animals available will, in general, be large. However, you may be able to breed them and use the young as seahorse food.

Freshwater shrimps are a good food for all seahorses, although they may not be suitable as a complete diet in and of themselves. They may be collected and kept in the same way as marine shrimps. Various tropical species are often offered for sale in the pet trade. Experimentation with breeding these shrimps may result in an important new food source for captive seahorses. If nothing else, you will no doubt enjoy keeping these fascinating creatures.

Amphipods are small, active crustaceans known locally as scuds, sideswimmers, or sand hoppers. At least 3,000 species occur in many saltwater and freshwater habitats, both along the shoreline and in the water. Land-dwelling forms, such as the rock hopper *Talitrus saltator*, often have legs adapted for jumping. Aquatic species, such as *Grammarus locusta*, are strong swimmers. Those dwelling in eelgrass beds resemble the plant to an uncanny degree and can be easily collected with a seine or dip net. Marine algae washed up along the shore often teem with amphipods. Marine species generally occur at higher concentrations than those in other habitats. However, the freshwater species *Grammarus fasciatus* is said to be extremely abundant in many commercial fish farms, so explore that option if it is open to you.

Amphipods, which seahorses of all types readily consume, provide an excellent source of nutrients. Freshwater forms will survive for some time in marine aquariums, but be sure to remove those that do not live. Also, note that the saltwater species are adept at hiding, so check that your seahorses are finding them.

Aquatic amphipods may be kept and bred in a filtered, well-lit aquarium. This will encourage the growth of algae. Females carry their eggs, numbering from 10 to 50, in a brood pouch. They can produce four to six clutches per year. Most species do well at temperatures of 70°F to 75°F (21°C to 23.6°C). However, you should check each species' natural range. Amphipods should be fed tropical fish food

TIP

You may wish to freeze excess marine shrimps and experiment feeding them to your seahorses.

flakes and trout chow. Various greens and dead fish are also good. A high-quality diet fed to food animals translates into healthier seahorses. Observing your amphipod colony should provide an interesting diversion—be sure to take notes, as people have much to learn about these creatures.

Brine shrimps, tadpole shrimps, and fairy shrimps: Although they superficially resemble tiny shrimps, these creatures actually comprise a separate order of crustaceans, the Eubranchipoda. Brine shrimps, *Artemia salina*, are 0.33 to 0.5 inch (0.8 to 1.3 cm) in length and reside in highly saline lakes. Dried eggs remain viable for years. The brine shrimps have thus become a staple of the live fish food industry. While eagerly accepted by nearly all seahorses, brine shrimps are inadequate as the sole diet of any except possibly the dwarf seahorse (*H. zosterae*). Even when being used for dwarf seahorses, you should supplement the brine shrimps' nutritional quality by allowing the shrimps to feed for two or three days. This is best accomplished by using a product such as Selco, algae pellets, or liquid foods designed for filter-feeding invertebrates (available at pet stores). Brine shrimps can form part of your seahorses' diet. However, if fed exclusively on them, your animals will languish and die in short order.

Mating pair of adult brine shrimp swimming among free eggs.

Brine shrimps can be hatched and reared in well-aerated seawater. Hatching time decreases as temperature rises, with an ideal time of 24 hours at 85°F (29.4°C). Eggs are readily available, so you do not need to breed brine shrimps. Adults can be purchased at most pet stores. Hatched eggs float, and the shrimps are attracted to light. Inverted soda bottles covered with black paper up to the bottle's neck will concentrate the shrimp at the bottom, near the cap, where they can be easily collected. The easiest culture method, however, is to use commercial shrimp hatcheries. With several operating at once, you will be assured of a supply of brine shrimps of various sizes.

Tadpole shrimp, *Triops* spp., are the freshwater parallel of brine shrimps in many ways. Some species are adapted to life in desert pools, where water may be available for a short period only once every three or four years. In such situations, the entire life cycle is completed in one week. Some populations are hermaphroditic. *Triops* cultures can be purchased from biological supply houses and generally survive in salt water long enough for the seahorses to discover them.

The closely related fairy shrimps (suborder Anastraca) may be collected in temporary freshwater pools. In temperate regions, they congregate in huge numbers in the late winter and early spring. This often occurs before other early harbingers of spring, such as wood frogs, have stirred.

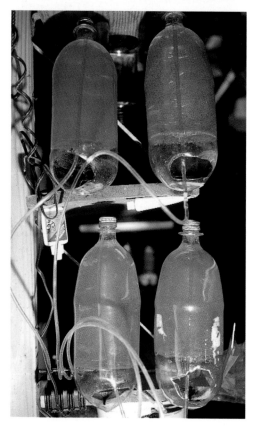

Hatching baby brine shrimp.

A breeding group of shrimp will provide important dietary variety.

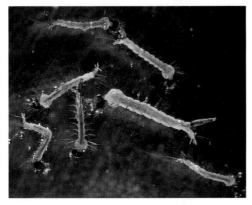

Mosquito larvae.

Blackworms.

Copepods, seed shrimps, water fleas, and plankton: Innumerable types of tiny crustaceans inhabit the world's fresh and salt waters. Many are valuable foods for captive seahorses. Collecting requires a fine-mesh net, such as the commercially available brine shrimp net or plankton net. Water fleas, or daphnia, can be collected in temporary pools and breed readily in captivity. The species *Daphnia magna* reaches a length of 0.25 inch (0.6 cm). At temperatures of 75°F to 80°F (23.6°C to 26.6°C), the females can produce 100 eggs every third day (with or without males), and sexual maturity is reached in eight days. Daphnia and the other creatures described below will thrive on algae tablets and liquid food for filter-feeding invertebrates. They should be housed in aquariums with a heavy growth of algae and with mild aeration. Due to their tiny size, water changes and a sponge filter should be used to clean the water.

Copepods, such as *Cyclops fuscus*, are small, maturing at a length of 0.125 inch (0.3 cm). More than 5,000 species inhabit the world's fresh and marine waters. Their bizarre lifestyles provide a lifetime of work for those inclined toward studying such creatures. The requirements for collecting and keeping them are similar to those described for daphnia.

Seed shrimps, or Ogtracods, are tiny crustaceans that scuttle about the bottom of freshwater and saltwater bodies. As they rarely swim, they may escape your seahorses' attention. However, they are well worth trying.

Seining with a fine-mesh net will yield an astonishing variety of tiny animals—generally termed plankton—that form the natural diet of seahorses. You must watch freshwater species carefully to determine their tolerance for salt water. A cause for concern when using saltwater species is the possibility of introducing fish parasites, such as fish lice (*Calgus* and *Argulus* spp.) into the aquarium. The value of nutritional variety, especially for such a sensitive animal as the seahorse, overrides the danger presented by parasites. This is especially true considering that parasites are fairly specific creatures in terms of their host. When collecting plankton, take time to examine your catch with a hand lens or microscope. Simply stated, you will not believe the treasure trove of bizarre minimonsters that you will encounter.

Bloodworms (*Chironomus* spp.) are actually the larvae of flying insects known as midges. Their red color is imparted by hemoglobin, the substance that carries oxygen in human blood. Bloodworms can be purchased commercially and stored in a damp container in a refrigerator. They are freshwater creatures and expire rapidly in salt water.

Black worms, microworms, grindal worms, and white worms: These animals are native to freshwater environments and do not survive long in marine aquariums. They are included in the spirit of experimentation. Black worms are available through the pet trade and should be stored in a moist box in a refrigerator. Microworms, *Anguillula silasiae*, are commercially available nematodes that may be raised in moist peat moss at a temperature of 75°F (23.6°C). They feed on moistened oatmeal. Grindal worms, *Enchytraeus buchholzi*, are related to earthworms and may be raised in a similar manner. The slightly larger white worm, *Enchytraeus albidus*, requires temperatures of 50°F to 55°F (9.9°C to 12.7°C). The widely available tubifex worm is an unsuitable food. It dies immediately upon contact with salt water and has been implicated in a variety of health problems when fed to other species.

Fish fry: Although not accepted by all seahorses, the young of easily bred tropical fish deserve some attention. Swordtails, platys, guppies, and mollies are all simple to maintain. They produce large numbers of live young. Black mollies and their relatives can be acclimated to salt water, and the fry will live until consumed. Do not, however, house adult mollies with seahorses—the former are efficient predators and will consume all food items before the seahorses are even aware that food is available. All of the fish mentioned may be housed in a ratio of one male to two or three females. They should be maintained at 73°F to 77°F (22.7°C to 24.9°C). Gravid females should be placed into a breeding trap, which is available at any pet store, to prevent them from consuming the young.

Frozen foods: Many of the food items previously discussed are available in the pet trade in frozen form. Therefore, acclimating your seahorses to frozen food is wise. This can be accomplished by mixing bits of frozen food in with the live food and gradually increasing the amount of frozen food offered. The food must, of course, be kept in motion by aeration or manipulation. The training process should begin when the seahorses are young. Acclimating seahorses to accept frozen food is a key step to establishing them for the long term. This will allow you to add such items as shrimps, scallops, mussels, clams, crabs, and fish to their diet. The food should be finely chopped and mixed, then frozen in thin sheets for easy handling.

Areas for Experimentation

Perhaps more than any other aspect of seahorse husbandry, the area of nutrition offers the hobbyist unlimited opportunities for experimentation. The huge tide of freshwater and saltwater invertebrates currently flooding the pet trade offers the possibility of procuring animals, especially shrimps, that can be bred at home. This could well change the face of seahorse husbandry at the private and professional level because satisfying the nutritional demands of seahorses is extremely difficult. The process of establishing new food sources is well worth the effort and is generally rewarding regardless of the outcome. Be sure to think in terms of creatures not generally thought of as seahorse food. Crayfish, for example, can be purchased at pet and bait stores or easily caught in commercial traps. Hundreds of tiny babies are produced (females carry the eggs until hatching). Since they are crustaceans, they may well be a nutritionally sound food item.

Seahorses are substantially less mobile than many other fish species, so you must observe your animals closely and learn their typical behaviors intimately. This will help you to recognize the subtle changes that may indicate a developing problem.

An Important Note Concerning Stress

When addressing the concept of the health of seahorses (or any other animal), understanding the role of stress is vitally important. A stressed animal can be made ill by microorganisms that it might fight off under other circumstances. The same applies to suboptimal captive conditions. Slightly poor water quality, for example, will be much more dangerous to a stressed than to a well-adjusted seahorse. This is one reason why so many captive animals of all types die in transit or soon after reaching their new homes. The chemicals released during the stress response are a necessary part of the seahorses' reaction to danger or the perception of danger. Long-term exposure to them, however (as occurs under conditions of poor husbandry), depletes or weakens the immune system and will leave the seahorses open to infection and disease. Because many diseases

A stress-free environment will go a long way in promoting good health.

and infection-causing agents are always present in a seahorse's body and environment, your pets must be subjected to as little stress as possible.

A poorly designed or overcrowded aquarium will be a significant source of stress for captive seahorses. Such conditions are all the more dangerous to animals that have been harvested from the wild. They are already in a weakened state from the ordeal of capture, shipping, and stays in any number of stops on the way to the dealer's shop. Seahorses forced to remain in the open or in closer-than-normal proximity to their neighbors will also decline in overall condition. A seahorse aquarium should be well planted and supplied with numerous hiding spots and sight barriers such as live rock, coral, and plastic and living marine plants. See page 19 for a description of the proper method of designing an aquarium for these delicate creatures. An insufficient supply of hitching areas will also evoke the stress response. Do not be misled into thinking that providing your seahorses with a complex exhibit and numerous hiding spots will deprive you of the ability to observe them. The exact opposite is true. Seahorses in a properly set up aquarium will show themselves often and engage in a variety of interesting behaviors never exhibited in a bare tank.

Improper temperatures and rapid fluctuations in temperature are common stressors of captive seahorses. You must research the appropriate temperatures for the species in which you are interested. Temperature fluctuations can be avoided by paying careful attention to your heater's operation and by installing a backup heater that will come on if the main one fails. Similarly, inappropriate or widely fluctuating pH and salinity levels should also be avoided at all costs.

Poor water quality is perhaps the most commonly encountered stressful condition in the marine aquarium. Be sure that you have a thorough understanding of filtration principles and water chemistry before attempting to establish seahorses in captivity.

Very active or aggressive tankmates of other species will be a source of stress even if they do not actually attack your seahorses. An animal that the seahorse normally encounters in the wild will take on a different perspective within the confines of an aquarium, especially if it is an active creature. Also, most fish will outcompete seahorses for food. Please see the chapter entitled "Seahorse Companions" for a description of suitable animals to include in the seahorse aquarium.

An improper diet is also a long-term and, unfortunately, very common stressful condition for captive seahorses. You are strongly advised against attempting to keep these fragile creatures unless you are able to meet their unique and demanding food requirements.

Signs of Illness

The telltale signs of specific ailments will be discussed under separate headings. Of importance, however, is to note the general behavioral signals indicative of the presence of disease, stress, or illness in seahorses.

Remember, as with all animals, appearing healthy is in each seahorse's best interest so it will not be singled out by predators. In other words, your seahorses may appear healthy when they are not. This makes the animal keeper's job all the more difficult and often results in illness being detected at an advanced stage, at which point treatment is more difficult.

You should note and understand your seahorses' routine behavior. Deviations from this behavior should send up a warning flag to you. Constant swimming may, for example, be indicative of poor water quality or of aggression by a tankmate. An increased rate of respiration may be due to inordinately high water temperatures (water holds less oxygen as the temperature rises), poor water quality, or parasitic infection. Lethargy and an unusual resting posture, like being unattached to an anchorage site, may also signal a problem. A reluctance to feed is also highly unusual. When these and other general symptoms are noted, you must identify the cause before administering medication. *If the problem is environmental, medication can do more harm than good.* Environmental problems are those that arise from outside the seahorse, like improper husbandry. You should carefully check all the aquarium inhabitants, water quality, and temperature readings as soon as you note a potential problem.

Seahorses are subject to many of the well-known ailments affecting other marine fish as well as several that are fairly specific. You must bear in mind that treatment for many of these has not been studied in depth. In this area, great opportunity exists for dedicated hobbyists to make real contributions. Draw upon your experience to experiment with a variety of treatments. Seek the advice of other aquarists and of professionals. Read as much as you can. Articles concerning other species may have relevance to your work with seahorses. Above all, publish and share your discoveries.

As is true for all captive animals, prevention of disease is best accomplished by sound husbandry practices and by quarantining all new animals for a three- to four-week period. See page 18 for a more complete discussion of quarantining procedures.

Please note that, when using any type of fish medication, you must read the label and the manufacturer's recommendations very carefully. Certain fish medications, especially those containing copper, are extremely toxic to marine invertebrates. Others may quickly kill off the beneficial bacteria in the filter bed. Activated carbon may filter medications out of the water quickly and render them useless. For these and other reasons, isolating the fish that is being treated is often easier than medicating the entire aquarium. Of course, the ailing seahorse must be housed in an appropriately furnished treatment aquarium. Placing such animals into bare, sterile tanks is tempting. However, in the case of seahorses, this will increase stress levels and may eliminate the value of the treatment protocol that you are following.

Parasites

Coral reef disease is a highly contagious disease caused by the protozoan *Amyloodium ocellatum*. It is fatal if left untreated. In its free-swimming stage, the parasite attaches to the fins, gills, and body of the seahorse and manifests itself as a network of tiny white and the yellow spots. Coral reef disease is highly contagious and affects seahorses as well as other marine fish. Symptoms include rapid respiration (due to gill involvement), often carried out near the water's surface.

Copper-based medications are used to treat this disease. The parasite forms a cyst during one portion of its life cycle and is immune to medication at this time. Treatment must therefore be continued for at least two weeks to be sure that all parasites have emerged from the cysts and are in the free-swimming stage. Be aware that copper is toxic to marine invertebrates in minute amounts. Using a copper test kit is also necessary to be sure that the levels stay within the treatment range. An overdose of the medication will also kill seahorses.

Saltwater ich (white spot disease) is caused by a protozoan (*Cryptocarya irritans*). It often takes hold during times of temperature stress, like after a period of rapid temperature fluctuation. It is often seen in animals held in a dealer's tank or shortly after purchase and establishment in the home aquarium. The protozoan's life cycle and the symptoms of infestation are similar to those for coral reef disease and are just as contagious. The attached parasites appear as white spots, larger than those caused by the coral reef disease protozoan. The life cycle of the protozoan means that 21 days of treatment are required to eradicate it.

Gas bubble disease: Grouped under this heading are a variety of maladies that afflict fish, amphibians, and reptiles as well as one specific to seahorses. Water supersaturated

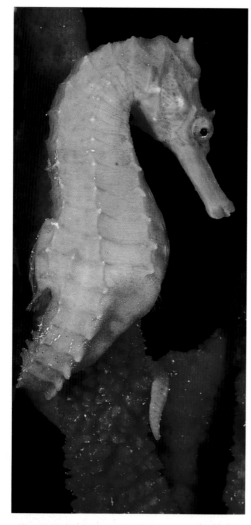

A well-fed seahorse at the peak of good health.

level. The enclosed air bubble can then be released by massage. The area should be treated with a bacterial medication designed for use with marine fish. Advanced cases are nearly impossible to treat and may be accompanied by external skin ulceration. Euthanizing an animal so afflicted is the best course of action. This can be humanely accomplished by using a commercially available euthanasia agent or by placing the animal, in a container of water, into the freezer.

A related ailment is gaseous buildup in the pouches of male seahorses. These animals cannot submerge and remain head down at the surface of the aquarium. Massaging the interior surface of the pouch with a pipette will expel the gas (keep the animal underwater while doing this). The pouch should then be flushed, via the pipette, with a marine fish antifungal medication. Continue the treatment until the symptoms disappear.

Clown fish disease, so named because clown fish are particularly susceptible, also strikes seahorses. The protozoan that causes the disease (*Brooklynella hostilis*) is not visible to the naked eye and spreads rapidly through the aquarium. Afflicted seahorses may die within one day of the onset of symptoms, which include skin lesions and rapid respiration. The animal's overall color may become pale, but this may not be visible in a seahorse that regularly changes color. The skin lesions associated with the condition provide a site for secondary bacterial infection, which further hastens the animal's demise. Malachite green-based medications are the treatment of choice.

with nitrogen or oxygen has been implicated in certain cases, although this is generally not a problem in aquariums housing seahorses. In any event, air bubbles appear under the skin and act as a staging area for bacterial infection. A sterilized needle can be used to open the area while the seahorse is held below water

Flukes are external parasites (trematode worms) that attach to seahorses and move freely from site to site. Their sharp, hooked mouth parts cause skin damage and lesions. Increased respiration, pale color, and rubbing movements (as the animal tries to dislodge the parasites) are signs of infestation. Many species of flukes are visible to the unassisted eye. A variety of medications, usually formalin based, can be used to eradicate flukes.

Copepods are parasitic organisms that are often specifically adapted to feed on one host species. They are visible to the naked eye and may attach anywhere on the seahorse's body. Females with their long strings of eggs resembling a forked tail are particularly easy to spot. The males die soon after mating and do not parasitize fish. A variety of medications is available to treat copepod infestations. As is true with many parasites, the eggs are immune to the medication. Treatment therefore must be extended until all eggs have hatched. In some species of copepod, this process may take as long as four or five weeks.

Fungi, Bacteria, and Viruses

These microorganisms are invisible to the unassisted eye. They are usually opportunistic invaders that establish themselves following injury or other trauma to the seahorse. The trauma may be stress or any other condition that weakens the seahorse's immune system. Various potentially harmful microorganisms are present in every aquarium, so you must take care to avoid situations that may cause an outbreak and allow them to become prob-

Good water quality is crucial to good seahorse health.

lematic. Parasitic infections frequently provide an opportunity for secondary infestation by bacteria, fungi, and viruses. If any of these conditions are present, you should check your aquarium's water quality, pH, temperature, and so on.

A fungal infestation may appear as a filmy coating or a dark area on the seahorse's body. You can treat it with a variety of fungicides, malachite green, or methylene blue.

Bacterial infestations are evidenced by ulcerations of the skin and the fraying or loss of fin tissue. These conditions have a variety of common names, such as fin rot or ulcer disease. A variety of antibiotics treats them. A bacterial infection nearly always indicates that another problem is present, often one in which another stress has compromised the seahorse's immune system. You should check your aquarium's water quality, pH, temperature, and so on and observe the interactions between tankmates. Please be aware that most antibiotics are toxic

to an aquarium's nitrifying bacteria. The death of these bacteria will cause a sudden, and often fatal, rise in ammonia levels. Treatment should, therefore, be carried out in a separate aquarium.

Viruses often follow an injury and are, at present, largely incurable. They manifest themselves as hard white nodules. Symptoms vary according to the virus involved and the organs affected. Hardy fish may survive mild infestations, but animals in obvious decline should be humanely euthanized. Commercial aquaculture texts may provide some insight into the treatment of certain viral outbreaks.

Diseases Related to Water Quality

Water quality problems, especially high concentrations of ammonia, are among the most common causes of marine aquarium failures. Even a gradual decline in water quality will stress your seahorses' immune system and open the animals to attack by bacteria, viruses, and fungi to which they may normally be immune. If you ignore the signs of poor water quality, the tank's population can be wiped out in a very short time.

Nitrogenous wastes: The levels of nitrogen-containing compounds in the aquarium greatly affect the health of marine animals, including seahorses. Of these, ammonia, nitrite, and nitrate are of most concern. For a more complete discussion of this topic, see page 25.

The most toxic nitrogenous compound found in aquariums is ammonia. Many marine invertebrates cannot tolerate even very low levels of this. At high levels, seahorses' ability to transport oxygen to their cells will be impaired. Seahorses under ammonia stress will breathe rapidly and become listless, occasionally sinking

to the bottom and failing to anchor to a holdfast. Secondary bacterial and fungal infections commonly occur.

You should perform an ammonia test at the first hint of a problem. A water change is the best way to deal with rising ammonia levels. Once the levels are acceptable, you must search for the cause of the problem. Common causes are overfeeding, a dead tank inhabitant, an improperly functioning filtration system, or a filtration system that is overdue for a substrate cleaning or a change. Ammonia levels may also rise if uneaten food or dead organisms are in the aquarium or if the aquarium is overstocked with animals. High ammonia levels are also common during the aquarium conditioning period, so you should not introduce seahorses at this time. Ammonia kits use varying ways of expressing the reading, so follow the enclosed instructions. Ammonia levels should not exceed 0.01 mg/L (or ppm).

Nitrite is less toxic than ammonia. However, fish vary in their susceptibility to high levels. Whether seahorses differ from other aquarium fish in their susceptibility to nitrite poisoning is not known. At sublethal levels, nitrite affects growth, inhibits reproduction, and also interferes with oxygen uptake. Many invertebrates are acutely sensitive to even very low concentrations of nitrite. If such animals are housed with your seahorses, they may die. The ammonia released by their bodies will add to the water quality problems. As with any water quality problem, you must determine the cause of the rise in nitrites. Nitrite levels should be held below 0.1 mg/L (or ppm).

As with nitrites, nitrate tolerance varies among fish species. Many invertebrates are sensitive to levels that do not trouble most fish.

Regular water changes are the best way to maintain and reduce nitrate levels. A healthy growth of marine algae will also help to prevent a spike in nitrate levels. Nitrate levels should not exceed 50 mg/L (or ppm). If live corals are kept, then 20 mg/L (or ppm) is a safe level.

Chlorine and chloramine are chemicals used by water authorities to purify water for human consumption. Both are toxic to marine organisms, with chloramine being the worse of the two. Chlorine is easily removed from water by using readily available dechlorination drops, which work instantly. Similar products are available to remove chloramine. However, a by-product of the chloramine detoxification reaction is ammonia, which is also highly toxic to marine fish. The ammonia therefore must also be removed before using the water. The easiest method is to place a box filter containing ammonia removers into the water. Then take a reading to ascertain whether the water is safe to use. Be sure to call your local water authority or supplier and ask what purification chemicals are used in the water you drink.

Heavy metals are toxic to most aquatic organisms. The one most commonly encountered by the aquarist is copper. It is often introduced by tap water that has passed through copper pipes. Such pipes are most common in older buildings. If your water passes through copper pipes, be sure to use a copper test kit to determine the copper levels present. Water from a copper pipe system may be rendered safe if you run it for 10 or 15 minutes before using it. Copper tends to accumulate when water lies in the pipes for long periods of time, for example overnight. The first water out of the pipe in the morning generally has the highest copper levels. You should

---

TIP

Seahorses under chlorine or chloramine stress generally become listless and sink to the bottom of the aquarium.

also consult your local water authority because some companies treat reservoirs with copper to control algae and parasites. Water with low but safe copper levels may be rendered unsafe when copper-based medications are used to treat ill fish (copper effectively kills a wide variety of invertebrate parasites and is a common component of marine fish medications). Be sure to test copper levels when using such medications.

Other heavy metals, such as aluminum and lead, may be present in rocks or aquarium ornaments. Using only farmed live rock is best. Rocks you collect, even from the ocean, may leach metals that will become a problem within the confines of the aquarium. Be certain that any plastic plants you purchase are specifically designed for marine aquarium use. Before using old plastic plants that you may have on hand, cut through the plastic to see whether a metal support bar is present. Some of the supports are extremely flexible and cannot be distinguished by a visual inspection.

The signs of heavy-metal poisoning in seahorses are, like other types of toxic reactions, general in nature. The most common reactions are lethargy and an increased rate of respiration.

Other toxins: Avoid spraying cleaners in the room where your aquarium is located. Glass cleaners, air freshners, and other commonly used household products become lethal when

A well-established and maintained aquarium can be breathtaking.

A male big-bellied seahorse showing the characteristically large brooding pouch.

introduced into the aquarium. Even if the aquarium is well covered, airborne chemicals can enter the water via the air pumps. If you must use chemicals in the room, disconnect any air pumps and use a submersible filter or power head for aeration. Be aware that aerobic bacteria in the substrate will die without oxygenated water, although the time frame for this is not well established. The room should be well ventilated with a fan before the air pumps are reconnected.

Nutritional Deficiencies

Nutritional deficiencies are a common problem for many species of marine fish and invertebrates. The problem is compounded because little is known about the requirements of all but the few well-studied species. Seahorses, with their very specific feeding requirements, pose one of the greatest challenges of all. Persuading captive animals to feed is often difficult. Those that feed may languish and die on a nutritionally deficient diet, such as the commonly used brine shrimps. Unfortunately, brine shrimps are the most readily available live food of suitable size that is available to most aquarists. The sheer magnitude of the food requirements of growing seahorses, as well as the lack of information concerning the natural prey of even the most common species, has long hampered breeding attempts. For an in-depth discussion of seahorse nutrition, see Nutrition and Feeding beginning on page 45.

A Word About Breeding Seahorses

As previously mentioned, the reproductive behavior of seahorses is unique among fish and, indeed, among all other animals as well. In addition to a remarkable strategy that includes male pregnancy, many species of seahorses mate for life. They reinforce their pair-bond with a complex ritual performed each day. This courtship display can last for over an hour. During that time, the pair changes color and spirals about an object gripped with their tails.

Male seahorses are easy to distinguish from females by their pouches. While some species, such as the dwarf seahorse, will reproduce in fairly small enclosures, most need sufficient space. The females of many species apparently require territories of up to 16 square feet (1.5 sq m).

While the home aquarist cannot usually provide such spacious quarters, every effort should be made to provide a suitably large enclosure. If the examples set by other fish species (and many other types of animals as well) are relevant, crowding will inhibit reproduction. Peaceful cohabitation is not necessarily an indication that population levels are satisfactory for breeding. To be safe, provide the largest tank possible to an individual pair of seahorses if breeding is your goal.

Many species of fish and other animals are keyed to reproduce by various environmental factors. Turtles native to temperate areas, for example, will generally not produce viable eggs unless they undergo a period of winter hibernation, complete with suitably lowered temperatures and a reduced period of daylight. Many amphibians will not even attempt reproduction unless stimulated by rainfall of the proper duration and temperature at the correct time of the year. Various fish species are spurred to reproductive activity by cycles of temperature and pH changes. Temperate-zone seahorses may be particularly sensitive to changes in the day length and in temperature because these are a natural part of their yearly cycle in the wild. Tropical species, which inhabit areas of fairly stable light and temperature levels, may nonetheless be subject to significant changes in pH and perhaps in salinity. These would be experienced by seahorses inhabiting shallow waters during the rainy and/or dry season.

As with many other aspects of seahorse husbandry, careful research is necessary to determine the factors that affect captive reproduction. You can easily manipulate temperature and daylight changes with thermostats and light timers. The best way to change salinity and pH levels is with very gradual water changes.

See page 11 for a description of the birth process in seahorses. The young require a large amount of food, up to 3,000 items per day for each animal in some cases. Newly hatched brine shrimps are the most readily available and commonly used food source. However, they are inadequate as a main diet, even if supplemented. Wild-collected zooplankton is the best food but is time-consuming to procure and difficult to maintain artificially. A colony of mysid shrimps is invaluable in the rearing process and should be established long before breeding commences.

Seahorse fry are best raised in bare-bottomed aquariums. The lack of a substrate allows the young fish to find their tiny prey more easily.

Although sufficient space for normal movement is required and many fish can become stunted in overly small enclosures, the seahorses must be surrounded by food at all times. A large tank stocked with too few food items will result in the seahorses slowly starving to death. Rocks with algae attached and plastic aquarium plants can be used as anchorage sites. The young of many seahorse species drift about for a week or so after birth, so do not be alarmed if they do not settle down right away. A sponge filter operated by a small air pump is the most satisfactory filtration system. Purchase a small chemical treatment cartridge to attach to the airlift tube. This will allow for some chemical filtration. However, be sure to check water quality regularly and make the appropriate water changes. As the young seahorses grow and gain strength, you can substitute a small corner filter for the sponge filter. Always be sure to avoid strong currents, which will stress the seahorses and interfere with feeding.

Once the seahorse fry are feeding, well established, and have gained some size, you should begin the process of training them to accept nonliving food items (see page 51). This process is easiest with young animals. Do not attempt it, though, until the animals are vigorous and have grown a bit. In most cases, this will be at age six weeks or later, but a variety of factors will have an effect. In no event should the fry be deprived of food during the process, which is more dangerous to young, growing animals than to adults.

CARING FOR THE VARIOUS SPECIES

The superficial similarity of many species of seahorse has generated a great deal of confusion in the aquarium trade and even among ichthyologists. In light of this situation, a number of characteristics are listed in the following pages that may be useful in determining the identity of your particular specimens.

Species Identification

Characteristics such as height of the animal and of the coronets (the raised area at the top of the head), the number of trunk and tail rays, the number of dorsal fin rays and pectoral fin rays, the form of facial and body spines, and permanent markings (as opposed to the very transient body coloration) are the easiest to use and are therefore those referenced. An excellent and far more detailed account of seahorse identification is given in *Seahorses: An Identification Guide to the World's Species and Their Conservation* (see Information, page 91). Except as where specifically noted, the seahorse species described in the following section will do best at the temperature, pH, and specific gravity levels described in the general discussions of those topics.

A variation of yellow seahorse (Hippocampus kuda).

Seahorse Species

Dwarf Seahorse, Hippocampus zosterae

Although better named *sea pony*, the diminutive dwarf seahorse barely reaches 0.9 inch (2.5 cm) in height. It is only slightly larger than the world's smallest species, the pygmy seahorse of Australia's southeastern coast. The little-known Lichtenstein's seahorse is the only other species in this size class.

The dwarf seahorse has 9 to 10 body rings and 31 to 32 tail rings. It has 12 dorsal fin rays and 11 to 12 rays in the pectoral fin. This seahorse can be yellow, all white, greenish, or darkly colored. It may be marbled with dark or white spots. Skin filaments are usually present but, for reasons not clearly understood, these are usually shed quickly when the animal is brought into captivity.

The dwarf seahorse ranges from Florida's Biscayne Bay on the east coast south to the

Bahamas and north to the waters off Pensacola, Florida. They are most commonly found in association with sea grass beds, especially *Zosterae* species, from which their Latin name is drawn. They frequent shallow waters.

The northern populations were formerly considered a separate species, *H. regulus*. In the natural state, dwarf seahorses are active by day. They have been observed moving about during all months except November, December, and January. The gestation period ranges in length from ten days to two weeks and is temperature dependent. The young, which can number from 3 to 25, are a mere 0.2 inch (7 mm) long at birth. Some evidence indicates that male dwarf seahorses are site-faithful.

The dwarf seahorse is a good aquarium animal, at least among such a delicate group of animals. Given their size, they can more easily be provided with the space necessary to establish almost normal-sized territories, an undertaking that is usually quite impossible where larger species are concerned. Take advantage of this and provide the largest aquarium possible—you will be rewarded with a much greater range of natural behaviors and with healthier animals. Keeping three pairs in a 15-gallon (55-L) well-planted aquarium will allow for naturalistic behavior and breeding. Most importantly, the dwarf seahorse is the only known species that can thrive on a diet consisting completely of

TIP

I recommend you purchase only captive-born seahorses.

enriched brine shrimps. Including other food items such as tiny rotifers and copepods would be prudent but is not absolutely necessary. One drawback concerning feeding is the incredibly small size of the fry—they can eat only day-old brine shrimps. You can easily overcome this handicap by using the culture methods described on page 47.

In the 1960s and early 1970s, dwarf seahorses were commonly sold via mail-order ads in the back of comic books. Although most undoubtedly met untimely ends, the huge public response did generate some attempts at commercial breeding.

Northern (or Atlantic) Seahorse, Hippocampus erectus

This large seahorse that grows to 7.3 inches (18.5 cm) nearly always causes surprise when it turns up in the shallow waters of North American's northeastern coast. Most people there consider seahorses to be tropical animals. The northern seahorse, however, resides in that area and indeed ranges as far north as southern Nova Scotia. Its huge range extends from southern Nova Scotia to Venezuela (a similar animal found further south may be a different species). The northern seahorse is the only species found north of North Carolina along the eastern coast of North America. South of that point, its range overlaps with that of the long-snouted seahorse and of the dwarf seahorse. It is most commonly encountered among floating masses of marine algae. It is often accidentally taken in crab traps and hauled in with algae attached to fishing lines.

A widely varying array of physical traits characterize the northern seahorse. This makes identification difficult and raises the possibility that additional species may eventually be described by ichthyologists. In general, the northern seahorse has 11 body rings and 34 to 39 tail rings. The dorsal fin contains 16 to 20 rays, and the pectoral fin has 14 to 18 rays. To complicate matters further, the coronet may be low and without spines, ridgelike, or raised and with either sharp edges or short spines. The spines themselves may be dull, sharp, or absent. Skin fronds are similarly confusing. Individual specimens may exhibit none, while those of others in the same habitat may be quite elaborate.

Although generally inhabiting sea grass beds in shallow waters, the northern seahorse has been taken at depths of over 230 feet (70 m). The author has encountered specimens being swept along by strong tides, attached to marine algae. Others report that this is not uncommon. Therefore, strict territories may not be held by populations living in areas subjected to strong tidal surges.

The northern seahorse is listed as *vulnerable* by the International Union for the Conservation of Nature and Natural Resources. It should not be collected. Commercial fishing for other species, and especially shrimp trawling, is likely causing severe population declines, especially in the southern part of the range. Many of the seahorses brought up as commercial fishing bycatch are funneled into the pet trade, where few survive due to the trauma of the collection methods.

Commercially bred specimens should be maintained with a light cycle typical of the area in which the animals originated. In the northeastern United States, specimens from the northern part of the range may be kept in an unheated aquarium near a window. A drop in temperature during the winter is beneficial.

FACT

Northern seahorse young, which can number up to 300, are born after a gestation period of approximately three weeks (depending on temperature).

This species is ideally kept by people living within its range so that natural food items can be collected and fed to it. This is an easier task than for some other species, as the northern seahorse's large size allows it to consume a wide variety of prey. It is also one of the few types of seahorse that may, with care and patience, be habituated to a diet consisting of nonliving food items. This will allow you to offer a greater variety of foods, which may avoid the nutritional deficiencies that so commonly plague captive seahorses.

Yellow Seahorse, Hippocampus kuda

Precisely describing the yellow seahorse is nearly impossible due to the wide variance in physical characteristics exhibited over the animal's enormous range. Specimens currently described as yellow seahorses have been collected from the western coast of India, throughout Southeast Asia, off Japan, along the northern coast of Australia, and along the far-flung islands of New Caledonia, the Solomons, Hawaii, and Tonga. Genetic research will likely determine that several species are currently described as yellow seahorses. Size and color are particularly troublesome as identifying characteristics. Some populations

mature at 2.7 inches (7 cm), while others grow to be as large as 6.7 inches (17 cm). The name yellow seahorse is quite misleading. In some areas, most specimens are black, while others are a sandy or white color. Those characteristics that tend to fall within roughly defined parameters include the 11 body and 36 tail rings and the 18 dorsal fin rays and 16 pectoral fin

Dwarf seahorses often anchor in close proximity to one another.

rays. The coronet is, in general, fairly low and is often topped by a slight depression. The spines are, in general, reduced to small, rounded bumps. Predictably, yellow seahorses appearing in the aquarium trade are routinely referred to as common, spotted, golden, giant, or brown seahorses. A well-developed ability to change color further complicates identification. In the pet trade of the United States and England, nearly all seahorses that lack spines and originate from the South Pacific are referred to as yellow seahorses.

The yellow seahorse is associated with nearly all inshore habitats that are suitable for seahorses. It has also been found attached to marine algae drifting in the open ocean. It is regularly collected in waters over 66 feet (20 m) deep.

The northern seahorse is often associated with eel grass.

Captive yellow seahorses do not usually exhibit the mate fidelity shown by many other species, but their social structure in the wild is largely unknown. The breeding season is, in some locales, associated with the rainy season. Gestation periods of approximately 30 days have been reported. However, this varies with temperature, as is true for all studied species thus far. Few generalizations can be drawn about brood size. As few as 15 and as many as 1,000 fry have been recorded.

The yellow seahorse is a mainstay of the aquarium trade. Wild populations are consequently under great collection pressure throughout the range. Therefore, you should choose only captive-born specimens for the aquarium. Selecting individuals from the larger-size races is also wise as these will accept a wider variety of food items. Also, the young are born at a larger size and are therefore easier to feed as well. As with any animal whose range encompasses a wide area, knowing the origin of your animals is important. This will allow you to fine-tune parameters such as temperature, specific gravity, and light cycles and is especially important if you are to achieve breeding success.

In addition to being important to the pet trade, the yellow seahorse has the dubious honor of being highly prized by practitioners of traditional Chinese medicine. It is also apparently harvested in India, again for medicinal purposes. The commercial value of this species and the multiple threats to its habitats render its continued existence shaky at best. Because it is so threatened, research into its life history and captive management is necessary.

A northern seahorse showing the
effectiveness of camouflage.

Barbour's Seahorse, Hippocampus barbouri

Barbour's seahorse is covered with sharp, well-developed spines. The longest is the first trunk spine, and up to five are found on the coronet. The tail spines vary in length. The long and short ones are usually arranged in an identifiable pattern. The eye spine is well developed.

Adults reach a length of 5.9 inches (15 cm), although some grow to no larger than 3.1 inches (8 cm). The double cheek spines and those below each eye are distinctive. They have 11 body and 35 tail rings. The dorsal fin has

between 16 and 22 rays, and between 15 and 20 rays are in the pectoral fin. Color is, in common with many seahorse species, not a reliable identification characteristic. Various individuals may be white, yellow, light brown, or any number of shades in between. Rust-colored dots and lines may be on the body, lines may exist on the snout, and thin lines may occur about the eyes.

This seahorse inhabits the waters between Malaysia and the Philippines. Although popular in the pet trade, little is known of the life history or the type of habitats Barbour's seahorses prefer. Since crucial information is lacking, proper captive husbandry is difficult if not impossible. Therefore, you should not purchase this species for home aquariums until field research can establish the physical parameters and diet necessary to maintain and breed it. This species was, for a time, shielded from collection for use in the traditional Chinese medicinal trade by its covering of spines. Smoother specimens were favored by practitioners of traditional Chinese medicine and especially by patients, who had a say in the choice of ingredients that went into their medications. One consequence of China's rapidly expanding economy has been an increase in the use of prepared traditional medicines. The seahorses in these are ground up before the purchaser sees them so that formerly unpopular species are now being collected along with the more traditionally desired types.

Big–Bellied Seahorse, Hippocampus abdominalis

The big-bellied seahorse is more readily identifiable than are many other types of seahorses. The body is much deeper (females have an especially deep keel) than that of other large seahorses. These also have more trunk rings (between 12 and 13), tail rings (between 45 and 48), and dorsal fin rays (between 26 and 29). At 12.5 inches (32 cm), it is the largest of the known seahorses. The spines are rounded, but those about the eye are very prominent. The coronet is low and triangular. The male's brood pouch is large and often colored white with a yellow border at the top. The animal is often brightly colored in shades of yellow, although white and brown specimens are not uncommon. Dark markings appear on the body, and alternating dark and light markings are on the tail. Males are readily distinguished from females by their greater number of dark blotches, longer tails, and shorter snouts. The males are heavier in weight while the females have a deeper keel.

The big-bellied seahorse is from cold waters, being found throughout the coastal areas of New Zealand and southeastern Australia. It has been encountered in sea grass beds, in rocky reefs, and near jetties.

Breeding occurs from October to January. After a gestation of approximately 30 days, the male gives birth to between 300 and 700 youngsters. The big-bellied seahorse has not been observed to form long-lasting pair relationships. However, much more needs to be learned about this animal.

Because it is protected by the Australian government, the big-bellied seahorse is not commonly seen in the pet trade. It is collected in New Zealand, with the majority of the catch being used by practitioners of traditional Korean medicine.

While its size may simplify feeding, the big-bellied seahorse requires cool water, 62°F (17°C). Providing this may be a problem for most aquarists. The author is not aware of attempts to habituate the animal to warmer water temperatures.

Thorny (or Prickly) Seahorse, Hippocampus histrix

The thorny seahorse has an extremely wide range, being found over a greater area than nearly any other species. The only other seahorse whose distribution approximates, in scale, that of the thorny seahorse is the great, or Kellogg's, seahorse. Of course, as with any little studied, wide-ranging animal, research may show that what is currently described as Kellogg's seahorse may, in actuality, be several species. Indeed, at least five other species have been classified as Kellogg's seahorse in the past. The situation is complicated, in typical seahorse fashion, by a great variety of individual differences in appearance among many populations and by the superficial similarity of quite distinct species.

Close examination will, however, reveal that thorny seahorses possess some unique physical characteristics that help distinguish them from other species. While almost all seahorses have more dorsal than pectoral fin rays, the number of pectoral fin rays (between 17 and 20) in the thorny seahorse equals or may even exceed the number of dorsal fin rays. The snout is very long. The most common body color is some shade of pale yellow. Pinkish and even green specimens, however, do occur regularly. The thorny seahorse draws its name from its extremely long, sharp spines. These spines are often tipped with a darker coloring than is found on the rest of the animal. The four or five long, sharp spines on the coronet and the one just before the coronet are distinctive. It

has a single cheek spine. Adult height ranges from 3.1 to nearly 5.5 inches (8 to 14 cm).

Specimens identified as thorny seahorses have been found off the coasts of Africa, Madagascar, Indonesia, China, Vietnam, Japan, New Guinea, Tahiti, and Hawaii. It is not often found in shallow waters and is most commonly collected at depths of over 19.6 feet (6 m). In contrast to the habitats inhabited by most other seahorse species, the thorny seahorse seems to favor areas devoid of algae, sea grass, and other cover.

The details of the thorny seahorse's life history are almost completely unknown. It rarely appears in the pet trade and should not be considered for the home aquarium until its habitats and natural history have been studied. The species is listed as *vulnerable* by the International Union for the Conservation of Nature and Natural Resources. The thorny seahorse has not traditionally been harvested for traditional Chinese medicine because spine-covered species have been considered undesirable. This situation is changing, however, as prepackaged and ground preparations are gaining wide acceptance in China. This species will likely face increased pressure from collectors.

Tiger-Tail Seahorse, Hippocampus comes

The tiger-tail seahorse may, at least in the case of darkly colored specimens, be readily distinguished from other species by its tail, which is banded in black and yellow. (The pattern may be difficult to distinguish in very dark specimens.) The body coloration is yellow with some shade of gray to black in alternating bands or other patterns. The spines vary widely from small, rounded knobs to large, well-developed

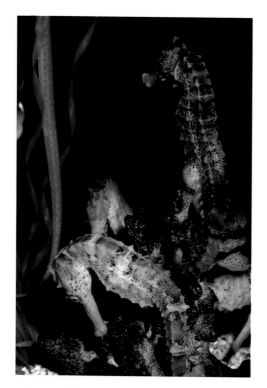

spikes. A dark marking often occurs near the tip. The tiger-tail seahorse has two cheek spines, two below the eye and occasionally two above the eye. The snout is long and sports a spine or knob at its base. The tiger-tail seahorse grows to nearly 5.9 inches (15 cm) in length.

The tiger-tail seahorse occurs in Southeast Asia along the coasts of Malaysia, Vietnam, and the Philippines. It is found in waters ranging from those that are quite shallow to those over 20 feet (6 m) deep. It is usually associated with corals, sponges, or floating algae.

The tiger-tail is nocturnal and spends the day within retreats in coral and other such hiding spots, which is unusual for a seahorse. It appears to be a territorial species, with one

Left: A trio of yellow seahorses.

Right: Another aptly named big-bellied seahorse.

pair continuously occupying the same area. In the Philippines, at least, courtship and breeding occur throughout the year. Up to 350 young are born after a gestation of between two and three weeks. As with most other species that have been studied, water temperature affects the gestation time.

Slender Seahorse, Hippocampus reidi

The slender seahorse has a long, blunt snout and lacks other body appendages such as

It's easy to see how the thorny seahorse got its name.

The slender seahorse can closely mimic its background.

filaments (cirri). True spines are lacking, and even rounded tubercles may be absent. The large coronet is rounded and often folded in upon itself. It has 11 body rays and 35 tail rays. Adults may measure as large as 7 inches (18 cm). Dorsal fin rays number between 16 and 19, and it has 15 to 17 pectoral fin rays. The cheek and eye tubercles are broad, and the snout is long and thick. Brown spots usually mark the body, and the tail is often heavily dotted in white.

The slender seahorse ranges from North Carolina on the eastern coast of the United States to the Caribbean and Gulf of Mexico. Specimens have also been taken off Brazil. However, further genetic research is needed to establish whether these truly are slender seahorses or a separate species. The slender seahorse inhabits water from 49 to 197 feet (15 to 60 m) deep. It has been taken attached to floating marine algae such as *Sargassum*.

Captive slender seahorses have reproduced in nearly all months of the year, but little is known of breeding behavior in the natural state. Observations of free-living animals indicate that they form exclusive pair-bonds. Brood size ranges from 200 to 1,600. The gestation is approximately two weeks, depending on water temperature. The International Union for the Conservation of Nature and Natural Resources lists the slender seahorse as *vulnerable*.

Black Seahorse, Hippocampus fuscus

The black seahorse, known as the sea pony in England, is usually black in color, but pale and even bright yellow specimens occur. Its color-changing abilities are well developed, so identification based on color is not reliable. Adults are 3.1 to 8.6 inches (8 to 22 cm) long, have 11 body rings, and 33 to 37 tail rings. The dorsal fin rays number from 14 to 17, and there are 14 to 16 pectoral fin rays. The coronet is low, as are the rounded spines. In overall appearance, the head seems very large for the size of the body.

The black seahorse inhabits the Red Sea and widely separated parts of the Indian Ocean (off the east coast of South Africa, along both coasts of Madagascar, and around most of Sri Lanka). Populations are widely separated. Whether other populations occur between the collection sites is not known. Specimens are generally found in shallow water up to a depth of 6.5 feet (2 m) or so, and they frequently inhabit sea grass beds.

Captive specimens are active during the day and form exclusive pair-bonds. They routinely engage in the typical seahorse greeting display (see page 11). The gestation time varies greatly with water temperature, with 14 days being average. Up to 130 young are born. Very little is known of behavior and reproduction in the wild.

The black seahorse is listed as *vulnerable* by the International Union for the Conservation of Nature and Natural Resources. It frequently appears in the pet trade and is harvested for traditional medicine in India. As a captive, the black seahorse may very cautiously be referred to as hardy, at least for a seahorse. Many, but by no means all, specimens will accept nonliving food. Larger-sized specimens are able to take a wide range of food items, which simplifies captive maintenance.

Long-Snouted Seahorse, Hippocampus guttulatus

A thick mane of skin fronds (cirri) sprouting all along the long-snouted seahorse's back gives rise to its alternate name, the many-branched seahorse. These thin structures branch at their tips, thereby providing excellent camouflage in the weedy areas favored by this species. Confusion abounds about its proper Latin name, with some authorities labeling the species as *Hippocampus ramulosus*.

The long-snouted seahorse is large, up to 7 inches (17.5 cm), although some populations mature at less than half this size. The dorsal fin is composed of between 17 and 20 rays. The pectoral fin contains between 16 and 18. The long-snouted seahorse's coronet is small and is topped by 5 bumps, and a spine is at its leading edge. It has prominent but blunt eye and body spines. The body color may be varying shades of light brown, gray, or green and is often marked with white spots circled by dark rings.

The long-snouted seahorse ranges into the quite cool waters of the eastern Atlantic Ocean, with the northernmost population reaching the Netherlands and the British Isles. It is considerably more common along the northern shore of the Mediterranean Sea and has been found as far west as Morocco and the Black Sea. A disjunct population off Senagal on

Africa's west coast may be a distinct species. Specimens from the most eastern portion of the range are also being examined in this light.

The long-snouted seahorse favors shallow waters and is generally found among plants such as eelgrass. The breeding season of the long-snouted seahorse extends from April through October. In the cooler reaches of its range, like the British Isles, gestation may last four to five weeks. Those inhabiting the warmer waters of the Mediterranean have a gestation period of approximately three weeks. The long-snouted seahorse is listed in the *Red Data Books* of France and Portugal and is classified as *vulnerable* by the International Union for the Conservation of Nature and Natural Resources.

European Seahorse, Hippocampus hippocampus

The European seahorse is another species that ranges into cold water, being found as far north as the Netherlands and in the English Channel. The European seahorse also ranges south to Spain and enters the Mediterranean Sea, where it occurs as far east as the coasts of Turkey and Egypt. A disjunct population off northwest Africa (Senegal and Guinea) and those in the Suez Canal area may be of another species, but the relationships are as yet unclear. As a fairly small animal, adult European seahorses mature at a size of 2.7 inches (7 cm) in length. The largest measure approximately 5 inches (12.5 cm). It has 11 body rings, between 35 and 38 tail rings, 16 to 19 dorsal fin rays, and between 13 and 15 pectoral fin rays. The coronet may be narrow throughout or narrow at the front and wide at the back. The European seahorse has one large eye spine, but all other spines are fairly low. The snout is very short, being less than one-third of the head length. The color of the European seahorse varies greatly, even for a seahorse. Individuals in the same geographic area may be gold, orange, purple, tan, brown, or black. The background color may be spotted with white.

The European seahorse is a creature of shallow waters, frequenting estuaries, bays, and rocky areas. The more northerly populations leave their feeding grounds for deeper waters during the colder months. Although the general breeding season extends from April through October, individuals from the northern reaches of the range limit reproductive activities to the warmer parts of the year.

The International Union for the Conservation of Nature and Natural Resources considers the European seahorse to be vulnerable. Portugal lists the species in its *Red Data Book*. It is not uncommon in the pet trade, especially in Europe.

Pacific Seahorse, Hippocampus ingens

The Pacific seahorse is a large species that grows to 7.5 inches (19 cm). It is the only one found along the Pacific coast of North and South America. The dorsal fin has 18 to 21 rays, and between 15 and 17 rays are in the pectoral fin. It has 11 body rings and between 38 and 40 tail rings. The color ranges from various shades of gray to brown, yellow, and gold. Reddish specimens also appear. The spines are not sharp. They may appear as small, rounded bumps or as prominent and well-developed spikes. The eye spine, which extends downward, is well developed with a blunt tip. The prominent cheek spine is also rounded at its end. The coronet is prominent and may be very high. The coronet sports raised areas that are, in contrast to the body spines, pointed at their tips.

The northernmost limit of the Pacific sea-horse's range is the waters off San Diego, California. From there the species ranges southward through the Gulf of California and along the coast of Mexico. Its southernmost distribution is off the coast of southern Peru.

The Pacific seahorse inhabits waters ranging from shallow inshore areas to those of approximately 66 feet (20 m) and has been taken at depths of 200 feet (60 m). In contrast to most other seahorses, the Pacific seahorse appears to be nocturnal. Captive specimens mature at one year of age and give birth to approximately 400 young after a gestation period of approximately two weeks.

The large body size and bright colors of the Pacific seahorse give it great popularity in the pet trade. It faces much pressure from collection, especially off Ecuador, where it is harvested for use in the traditional Chinese

Left: A close-up on the head of a slender seahorse.

Right: The Pacific seahorse (H. ingens).

medicine trade. Many thousands also perish in the nets of commercial shrimp trawlers. Dried animals are sold as curios throughout the southern part of the range. The Pacific sea-horse is listed as a *vulnerable* by the International Union for the Conservation of Nature and Natural Resources.

Golden (or White's) Seahorse, Hippocampus whitei

Although it often sports a beautiful golden color, this seahorse may also be brown or shades of mottled gray. As a small species, adults range in size from 2.4 to 5.1 inches (6 to 13 cm) and possess 11 body and 32 to 36 tail rings. It has between 16 and 20 dorsal fin rays and between 15 and 18 pectoral fin rays. The snout is quite long. The eye and cheek spines are well developed and sharp. The other spines vary greatly in appearance. They may be low and rounded, moderate, or long and pointed. The high coronet is topped by 7 sharp spines.

The golden seahorse is found off the eastern coast of Australia and along the Solomon Islands. It is most commonly encountered in shallow waters, although specimens have been collected at depths of 82 feet (25 m). It is nearly always associated with dense cover and favors eelgrass beds, sponges, and artificial structures such as docks and jetties.

In typical seahorse fashion, the golden seahorse is active by day. Pairs appear to form long-lasting, exclusive bonds. Gestation takes up to three weeks (longer at cooler temperatures), after which 90 to 250 young are born. Courtship and breeding have been observed from October through April in free-living animals.

As of 1998, collecting Australian specimens is prohibited by the Australian Wildlife Protection Act. The golden seahorse is classified as *vulnerable* by the International Union for the Conservation of Nature and Natural Resources. The Solomon Islands population is unprotected, and little information is available about commercial pressures.

Knobby Seahorse, Hippocampus breviceps

Several unusual physical characteristics combine to confer a quite bizarre appearance to the knobby seahorse. The snout appears short

The knobby seahorse (**H. breviceps**).

and the tail long in proportion to the small body size (adult specimens are a mere 1.7 to 3.1 inches (4.5 to 8 cm). The snout is also upturned very slightly at its end. Many individuals sport thick skin fronds along the head and neck, giving the appearance of a horse's mane. The brood pouch of the mature male is also out of proportion to the body size, being quite large. Gravid specimens are consequently very noticeable. The knobby seahorse has 11 body rings and 40 tail rings. It has between 19 and 23 dorsal fin rays and between 13 and 15 rays in the pectoral fin. The coronet is high for such a small animal and may be a round bump or columnar in shape. In contrast to many species, the spines of each individual vary in appearance throughout the body. The body color is generally brown and tinged with purple or some shade of yellow through red. Specimens of all color phases exhibit dark-ringed white spots throughout the body. The head is often mottled with dark patches. Light-colored stripes traverse the tail's dorsal surface.

The knobby seahorse is generally encountered in sea grass beds, along coral reefs, or attached to floating marine algae. The range of the knobby seahorse extends along the western coast of Australia and along the southern coast to the area of Port Philip Bay in Victoria. It also occurs all along the coast of Tasmania. Specimens from the western portion of the range differ from those in the east by having proportionately longer snouts. These may represent a separate species, but genetic research is needed.

Details of the life history of the knobby seahorse are largely unknown. Australia granted this species protection in 1998 under the Australian Wildlife Protection Act. The International Union for the Conservation of Nature and Natural Resources lacks sufficient data to classify the animal with a specific designation.

The knobby seahorse's unusual appearance increases its desirability in the pet trade. Due to the nearly complete lack of basic information about its natural history and captive requirements, home aquarists should not keep this species.

Pygmy (or Bargibant's) Seahorse, Hippocampus bargibanti

The pygmy seahorse, as its name suggests, is one of the smallest seahorse species. It is also one of the most unusual among a group for which unusual is the norm. The species was not described until 1970. The pygmy seahorse bears an amazing resemblance to the gorgonian (a soft coral) on which it lives. The only place it has ever been observed or collected is attached to one of two species of gorgonian coral of the genus *Muricella*. So closely does the pygmy seahorse match its host coral that it came to light only after the coral had been collected and was established in an aquarium! The snout and body tubercles are shaped and colored to match the polyps of the host gorgonian exactly. The body form mimics that of the gorgonian's stem. Two color phases have been identified, each of which matches a particular species of gorgonian coral. One is gray or purple in color, with pink to red tubercles on the body. This variation lives in association with the species *Muricella plectana*. The other color morph is yellow with orange tubercles and attaches itself to the gorgonian coral *Muricella paraplectana*.

The uniqueness of the pygmy seahorse's appearance is heightened by its near lack of a protruding snout so typical of other seahorse species. The mouth itself is situated just barely out from the eyes. The animal appears cut off in silhouette, even when compared with other short-snouted species.

True to its name, the adult pygmyy seahorse measures less than 0.8 inch (2 cm) in height. It has 11 or 12 body rings and 31 to 34 rings in the tail. Dorsal fin rays number between 13 and 15, and the pectoral fin contains 10 rays. The body rings are faint. The animal appears soft and fleshy as opposed to the stiff appearance of other seahorses. This seems to be an adaptation to allow the animal to blend in effectively with the host gorgonian coral. The only spines, per se, are the single rounded eye spine and the one cheek spine. The body spines take the form of bulbous tubercles, again aiding in camouflage by mimicking the host's polyps. The coronet is low and rounded.

In addition to being found only at a very specific attachment site, the pygmy seahorse is, as far as is known, restricted to waters ranging in depth from 52 to 131 feet (16 to 40 m). It has been collected in widely scattered locales—off Sulawesi (Celebes) Island in Indonesia, at the tip of Papua New Guinea, on Australia's Great Barrier Reef, and along the coast of New Caledonia. Its size, apparently sessile lifestyle, and extremely sophisticated camouflage raise the likelihood that the information concerning its range is far from complete.

Limited observations indicate that monogamous pairs may form. Strangely, however, groups of apparently paired animals have been found on single gorgonian corals. Such clustering may increase the effectiveness of the species camouflage, as is the case with other types of widely different animals. However, this is pure speculation at this point.

The pygmy seahorse is protected by the Australian government under the Australian Wildlife Protection Act. Insufficient information exists to warrant classification by the International Union for the Conservation of Nature and Natural Resources. The extremely specific requirements of this animal render it vulnerable to habitat destruction or collection. Its uniquely shaped snout and habitat also raise the possibility that it relies on very specific food items and would therefore fare poorly in the face of environmental change.

Sea Dragons

These fantastically shaped relatives of the seahorse are native to the cool waters of southern Australia. Two species exist: the leafy sea dragon, *Phycodurus eques*, and the weedy sea dragon, *Phyllopteryx taeniolatus*. An array of flattened, leafy appendages grants them an

FACT

Future Finds?

The recent discovery of the unique pygmy seahorse raises speculation about the existence of other, as yet undiscovered, seahorse species.

incredible degree of camouflage. Their flattened bodies can be up to 18 inches (45 cm) in length. They appear even larger because of their elaborate, leafy outgrowths.

Males incubate up to 250 eggs in brood pads on the undersides of their tails. The eggs are not enclosed in a pouch but are held in place by a sticky substance secreted by the male.

The seahorse fancier should make every effort to see these fantastic creatures. They are rapidly gaining popularity in public aquariums in the United States, with at least 14 institutions exhibiting them as of 2001. In 1995, in contrast, only the Dallas World Aquarium had them. Public aquariums are the only place to see them—they are not available to hobbyists because Australia protects them.

Their requirements in captivity include mechanically chilled water and huge numbers of live mysid shrimps. Some aquariums, however, are experimenting with frozen food.

Sea dragons have not yet reproduced successfully in captivity. In May 2000, a male on display at the Long Beach Aquarium of the Pacific (near Los Angeles, California) carried 100 eggs for five weeks. Several young hatched prematurely, and the male died shortly thereafter.

Seahorses are, by their nature, unsuited to life in a community aquarium. In addition to being extremely finicky eaters, they are, in general, sit-and-wait predators. As such, they are not adept at searching out food. Instead, they wait in ambush, aided by their excellent camouflage, for small creatures to venture close by.

Unsuitable for Aquariums

In an aquarium housing actively swimming fish, all food will be long consumed before the seahorses even know that feeding time has come. The problem is exacerbated because the foods consumed by seahorses, such as small, live invertebrates, are the favorites of nearly all aquarium fish. Even typically vegetarian species relish tiny, living food items. Also, seahorses rely on camouflage for defense. This does not, however, protect them within the confines of an aquarium. They suffer from the aggressive attention of even the most docile marine species.

This having been said, a surprising variety of fish and invertebrates can, with careful atten-tion, be safely housed with seahorses. Please do not attempt to establish a mixed-species aquarium until you have had a good deal of experience maintaining seahorses by them-selves. These delicate creatures are difficult enough to care for without the added stress

Invertebrates such as shrimp can be suitable seahorse companions, but keep them in pairs.

and competition imposed by other creatures. When you are well experienced, you might wish to consider some of the marine animals discussed in this chapter. You can choose from an unlimited diversity of creatures. Use the following discussion as a guideline, and begin experimenting with species similar to those highlighted here. Eventually, you may want to come up with your own ideas. As always, the key is research, discussion with experienced professionals and hobbyists, and careful observation.

When adding specimens to the seahorse aquarium, be aware that normal (and possibly aggressive) behavior will likely not be exhibited during the first few hours or even days of the introduction. Do not be lulled into a false sense of security by an animal that appears shy and retiring when first placed into the tank. As the specimen adjusts to the water chemistry and other aspects of the new habitat, its true nature will be exhibited. Watch new animals closely. Consider installing a plastic divider if you will be away for long periods of time early in the introduction process.

Acceptable Aquarium Companions

Pipefish belong to the same order (Syngnathiformes) as seahorses and share with them an elongated snout and heavily armored body. Their method of swimming, reproduction, and feeding is also similar to that of their near relatives. All pipefish are confirmed live-food specialists. Over 200 species of pipefish inhabit the earth's tropical and temperate seas, most often in shallow water near cover. They resemble various marine plants, such as eelgrass, to a remarkable degree. Many types even orient themselves to blend in perfectly with the position of the blades of eelgrass or other plants. Various species of pipefish are also found in the open sea, usually in association with floating marine algae. A few types have even colonized freshwater environments, something that their seahorse cousins have yet to do.

Those who seek to keep pipefish in captivity are faced with challenges similar to those posed by seahorses, especially as regards feeding. Pipefish are somewhat more active than seahorses. They also appear to be more alert in their feeding response, so be certain that the pipefish do not compete with your seahorses at feeding time. Most require densely planted aquariums and particularly favor eelgrass or plastic plants with thin, upwardly oriented leaves.

The northern pipefish, *Syngnathus fuscus*, occurs in sometimes surprisingly high densities among the eelgrass beds of the eastern coast of the United States. It makes a fairly hardy captive. It does well on a diet consisting mainly of nutritionally supplemented brine shrimps with other suitably sized invertebrates offered on occasion.

Average room temperatures suit it well, and a cool period in the winter is beneficial.

The banded pipefish, *Doryrhamphus dactyliophorus*, is occasionally offered in the pet trade. It is strikingly marked with alternating bands of black and yellow. It does best on a diet of supplemented brine shrimps and other typical live foods recommended for seahorses. The author has not had success in conditioning either of the aforementioned species to accept nonliving food items, although others have reported that such is possible.

Gobies belong to one of the largest families of fish, with over 2,000 species recognized and up to 25 new ones being described each year. They range the world's marine environments, and some have also colonized freshwater. Most are small. In many, the ventral fins are fused into a cuplike disk. This allows the gobies to cling to the various substrates around which they spend their time. While some are active swimmers, most live along the bottom or around rocks or other cover. They move about with a scurrying motion and are almost rodentlike in their actions.

It is their habitat preference that suits some for consideration as seahorse companions. Although they favor live food, most are reluctant to leave the security of their retreats (many dig or appropriate burrows or other shelters) and are therefore less likely to compete with seahorses for food. Certain bold individuals will, however, abandon their secretive ways and swim in the aquarium's upper levels at feeding time. Therefore, you must closely monitor each individual's behavior. One trick is to drop a favored food item, such as a clump of black worms or a shrimp pellet, in front of the goby and allow it to feed before introducing food for the seahorses.

Certain goby species feed largely upon algae and are occasionally sold in the pet trade. These are good choices for inclusion in the seahorse aquarium. However, most will take some live food as well, so they must be watched. Tropical gobies are often quite colorful, and many species are readily available. Be sure to consult your supplier for information about the ultimate size and food preference of the species you are considering.

The bumblebee goby, *Brachygobius doriae*, is a brackish-water species from southeast Asia but can be acclimated to a fully marine aquarium. It is, like its namesake, attractively colored in black and yellow and is reluctant to leave the substrate for food. This species can become a notorious fin ripper, so watch these individuals carefully.

The naked goby, *Gobiosoma bosci*, is native to the Atlantic coast of the United States. It scuttles about the bottom, returning to its shelter after each short foray and peering out in a most entertaining manner. It also rarely swims above the substrate level in search of food. Like most gobies, males guard eggs attached to the sides of a shelter. The young can be reared on finely chopped black worms and brine shrimps. Naked gobies may be collected by seining through eelgrass beds or by checking shelters such as discarded tin cans. Be sure to check local regulations before collecting. They are not sold in the pet trade.

Flatfish: A variety of immature flounders, such as the fluke—*Paralichthys dentapus* and the hog choker—*Trinectes macurotus*, may be seined in eelgrass beds from areas where this is legal. Their bizarre body form and incredible ability to match their surroundings renders them fascinating aquarium subjects. Other species are occasionally offered in the pet trade, usually marketed as *freshwater flounders*. Most are actually brackish-water species that can be slowly acclimated to marine aquariums. The flatfish often refuse all but live food but will feed readily on commercially available sandworms or small shrimps. They will not leave the bottom to compete with seahorses for food. One drawback is that most species grow large enough to consume or at least injure seahorses, so they should be transferred to a more suitable aquarium as they increase in size.

Sticklebacks, so named for their protruding dorsal-fin spines, are small freshwater and marine fish. Males use an adhesive, manufactured in the kidneys, to construct an enclosed nest of vegetation. Females are induced to lay their eggs within by a highly ritualized courtship display.

Sticklebacks are probably related to seahorses. Although more alert feeders than their relatives, stickleback appetites are small and easily satisfied. They may thus be fed before the seahorses so as to allow the slower animals to feed undisturbed. Sticklebacks prefer live food, but many will accept fish flakes and small pellets. A pair of smaller ones such as the three-spine stickleback, *Gosterosteus aculeatus*, will do no harm when housed with larger, temperate-zone seahorses such as the Atlantic seahorse, *Hippocampus erectus*. Be sure to provide closely spaced, upright supports and live vegetation for nest building, as many species adapt well to captivity and may breed. Sticklebacks can become violently territorial, particularly during the breeding season, so you must monitor them carefully.

Banded coral shrimps and other shrimps: Banded coral shrimps, *Stenopus hispidus*, are a

A turban snail.

brilliant red and white in color and are not shy about foraging in the open. They establish long-term pair-bonds, and males have been observed sharing food with gravid females. The eggs are carried on the swimmerets. However, the tiny young must be removed because adults (and large seahorses) will consume them. Banded coral shrimps are inoffensive toward tankmates and feed upon chopped shrimps, commercial pellets, flake foods,

Leather corals and soft corals, like the African bush (Lemnalia africana), are hardy aquarium dwellers.

and algae. They should be kept in pairs if possible and, like most invertebrates, are extremely sensitive to changes in water quality and many medications.

A huge array of marine shrimps are suitable for aquariums housing sea-horses. Tropical species are often brilliantly colored. Only those large types

Hermit crabs are fascinating and inoffensive.

The bizarre brittle star will consume uneaten food in the aquarium.

Starfish in captivity can be induced to accept bits of clam meat.

A number of sea urchin species are available (above and right).

with powerful claws pose any danger to sea-horses. Tiny species such as grass shrimps, *Palaemonetes* sp., and sand shrimps, *Crago septemspiosus*, may be collected with seines. A colony installed in the aquarium will be a source of endless entertainment with their constant foraging and interactions. Larger seahorses will consume smaller shrimps, and well-kept shrimps will breed in the aquarium. Their young are an important food for captive seahorses.

Shrimps perform a valuable service in the aquarium by consuming uneaten food and other wastes. They will also take flake, frozen, and pelleted foods as well as small live-food items and algae. Most will also relish occasional bits of meat, chopped shrimps, and fish.

Hermit crabs: Many small hermit crab species, such as the long-clawed hermit crab, *Pagurus longicarpus*, make delightful exhibit animals. These hardy crustaceans are constantly in motion—feeding, squabbling over territories, and trying on new shells. (Hermit crabs use the abandoned shells of other sea creatures as homes in which to live and seek larger quarters as their bodies grow.) Some tropical species grow large enough to damage seahorses, but smaller ones are quite harmless. They will consume a wide array of commercial fish foods and algae, and they are valuable scavengers. Also, occasionally offered for sale are species that will attach a sea anemone to the shell as protection or camouflage. The host crab will move its anemone guest each time it changes shells. Hermit crabs of various species may be collected in tidal pools or by seining along shorelines. Be sure to include extra empty shells for the crabs to use as they grow.

Spider crabs: Over 600 species of these bizarre decapods exist. The largest is the Japan-ese giant spider crab, with a leg span of 8 feet (2.5 m). The species commonly encountered along the Atlantic coast of the United States, the Atlantic spider crab, *Limbinia emarginata*, is ideally suited to aquarium life when young. Larger specimens are not a danger to seahorses because their claws are tiny and they are not aggressive. However, their lumbering movements will stress their delicate tankmates (unless housed in an extremely large aquarium). Immature Atlantic spider crabs place algae, or whatever else they can find, into the crannies of their carapace. The camouflage effect is readily apparent, as the animals take on the appearance of a moving plant. The author has also observed them picking and nibbling at this portable garden from time to time. They readily use kale and other plant material in this activity. Spider crabs forgo this habit once they attain a size of 3 inches (7.5 cm) or so, for reasons as yet unknown.

Atlantic spider crabs may be collected in tidal pools and eelgrass beds. Their appetites are easily satisfied with commercial fish flakes, pelleted fish food, greens, algae, and black worms. They seem to be possessed of a suicidal impulse to leave the aquarium for dry land at night, so be sure that your tank is tightly covered.

The closely related arrow crab impales extra food, such as a piece of shrimp, on its pointed snout. (Actually, the snout is an extension of the carapace.) It carries the food around until hunger strikes. This odd creature is readily available in the pet trade and is inoffensive toward seahorses.

A wide variety of other crabs may be collected or purchased. In general, swimming crabs (those with the rear legs flattened into paddlelike shapes) are aggressive creatures that will kill seahorses and other tankmates. Even quite small specimens exhibit surprising ferocity. Stay with small-clawed, slow-moving species such as the various spider crabs.

Starfish, brittle stars, and sea urchins: The more typical of the echinoderms, such as the common sea star, *Asterias forbesi*, are familiar to most folks. However, a huge variety of less commonly seen forms exist as well. Sea stars feed upon clams and other mollusks in the wild. They will eagerly take bits of clam, shrimps, and other such foods in captivity.

The bizarre brittle stars react quickly to the scent of food by crawling about the substrate with their slender arms exploring every nook and cranny. They will accept all manner of frozen and pelleted fish foods.

Sea urchins will consume a wide variety of frozen and pelleted fish foods. They orient the movable spines to shadows passing overhead to present a barrier to potential predators. Beware of these spines when handling sea urchins, as many forms possess venom glands and the chemistry of the venom has not been well studied. These creatures exist in an enormous variety of species, many of which can be easily collected. Tropical forms are regularly offered for sale as well.

Marine snails are some of the most abundant animals in certain habitats. The number of forms in existence is truly staggering. Many make hardy and inoffensive tankmates for seahorses. The periwinkle, *Littorina littorea*, is European in origin but has been introduced to the Atlantic coast of the northeastern United States. It is a fine scavenger, consuming both plant and animal material. Mud snails, *Nassa obsoleta*, remain below the substrate until food is scented, at which time all will emerge and head unerringly in the right direction. A wide array of colorful tropical snails is also regularly offered for sale in the pet trade. Most marine snails feed upon algae, green vegetables, fish flakes, and fish pellets. All appreciate an occasional treat in the form of a bit of clam meat or fish.

Tube worms attach their thin, white, tube-like shelters to rocks or other solid supports. The feeding appendage, which is extruded from the tube, is flowerlike and in many species is quite beautifully colored. Tube worms often arrive unnoticed in the aquarium as inhabitants of live rock. All are filter feeders and do well on commercially available foods formulated for such creatures.

Corals: Keeping live corals is a specialized and rapidly developing field within the discipline of marine animal culture. Be sure to purchase only farmed specimens, as coral reef destruction is a major environmental concern. There is little to compare to the beauty of the aquarium containing live rock and live corals in addition to seahorses. Many corals provide ideal hitching areas and shelters for seahorses. The captive husbandry of corals is beyond the scope of this book, but a wide variety of specialized titles is available. Please be sure to research carefully—the keeping of live corals is quite different from the culture of other marine invertebrates.

SEAHORSE SURVIVAL

Most people know about the decline and outright collapse of marine fisheries worldwide and the hardships faced by people who depend on the fisheries for their livelihoods. Less well publicized is the plight of one of the most beloved and unique of all fish, the seahorse.

Environmental Ethics and the Law

In contrast to the threats facing most other fish, seahorses are plagued by a perceived medicinal, rather than culinary, value. At the bare minimum, 20 million per year are used in traditional Chinese medicine. Millions more are sold as (usually short-lived) aquarium fish and dried curios.

Survival: The bleak outlook for their continued survival is compounded by the fact that seahorses dwell, for the most part, in the marine habitats most affected by human activities—coastal sea grass beds, estuaries, mangrove swamps, and coral reefs. Pollution, land reclamation, industrial development, and the introduction of exotic species are all particularly devastating to inshore marine communities. In addition, the fate of seahorses is linked with that of other commonly exploited species. Many seahorses are accidentally caught by trawlers searching for edible fish.

The seahorse's tail is highly prehensile (yellow seahorse, H. kuda).

Danger: Any species can be placed in jeopardy by human activities. However, seahorses are particularly vulnerable. Since they are fairly sessile—unable to move quickly—they cannot recolonize rapidly. Also, their unique pair-bonding (see page 11) indicates that their reproductive process is very susceptible to disturbance. People who work with seahorses are noting enormous declines in the populations of many species. Therefore, people who keep seahorses must be certain that their specimens are captive bred. Hobbyists must also study the literature so they can breed seahorses. Much of the necessary work can be carried out at libraries, aquariums, and museums.

The state of the environment today is such that each animal removed from its natural habitat does make a difference. Every time another species becomes extinct, it affects other plants and animals. Each extinction closes a door on possible cures for disease that may be locked away in the body chemistry of the extinct creatures. The author's work at the Bronx Zoo/Wildlife Conservation Park and Staten Island Zoo has convinced him that serious hobbyists can make a difference by cooperating with similar institutions and by not disturbing natural populations of seahorses. If and when collection is necessary, it should occur through conservation organizations and under strict government supervision.

Disappearing species: The increased focus on disappearing species and the explosion in collecting wild animals has led to the passage of local, state, and federal laws to protect many species. The fact that an animal is in a pet store does not mean that it is legal to purchase it. The prospective seahorse owner is responsible for researching the legality of seahorse ownership.

Medical Research

Seahorses have been an accepted part of traditional Chinese medicine for hundreds of years. This form of medicine and its offshoots date back over 2,000 years and are used by at least 30 percent of the world's population. Unless proven groundless, such practices should not be attacked per se. Instead, efforts should be put into sustaining populations of potentially useful seahorse species. Research supporting the medicinal value of seahorses should be used as an impetus for conservation, not exploitation of wild populations. If you are interested in medical research and conservation, a more worthwhile project would be hard to find. Research into environmentally sound alternatives to seahorse collection is also desperately needed.

Contributions You Can Make

As mentioned previously, cooperation with aquariums, museums, and other institutions can provide serious hobbyists with the opportunity to indulge their passion while helping preserve wild seahorse populations. Such cooperation can include participating in breeding programs, field studies, release programs, or surveys. Of course, any activities that result in environmentally sound legislation will benefit a variety of creatures, including seahorses. The Florida Aquarium has implemented a program to survey and study local seahorse populations. Project Seahorse works to ensure the survival of seahorses while respecting the needs of those who rely on these creatures for their livelihoods. Led by Amanda Vincent of McGill University and Heather Hall of the Zoological Society of London, the organization supports conservation efforts in the Philippines, Hong Kong, and Vietnam. Project Seahorse can be reached at *www.seahorse.mcgill.com*. One important step that you can take is to participate in the seahorse biology, trade, and medicinal surveys sponsored by this group.

You should also support marine conservation by promoting appropriate educational and governmental activities and the development of alternatives to seahorse collection as a living. If you must purchase seahorses, please make an effort to determine that they are captive bred. If you make medicinal use of these creatures, learn which are captive bred or are harvested from sustainable populations and purchase those only. Please also research alternatives. Finally, recognize that seahorses are harmed by humans who trade in other marine species. Therefore, refuse to buy fish from poorly managed fisheries. An excellent guide to choosing environmentally sound, edible fish is the *Seafood Lover's Almanac* by Mercedes Lee.

Useful Literature

Books

Goldstein, R. *The Marine Reef Aquarium Handbook*. Hauppauge, NY: Barron's Educational Series, Inc., 1997.

Lee, M. (ed.). *Seafood Lover's Almanac*. Islip, NY: National Audubon Society's Living Ocean Program, 2000.

Lourie, S. A., A. C. J. Vincent, and H. J. Hall. *Seahorses: An Identification Guide to the World's Species and Their Conservation*. London: Project Seahorse, 1999.

Moe, M. A. *The Marine Aquarium Reference*. Plantation, FL: Green Turtle Publications, 1993.

Straughan, R. P. L. *The Salt Water Aquarium in the Home*. New York: A. S. Barnes and Co., 1970. (Note: Do not be put off by the publication date—this book is packed with original observations about an enormous variety of marine creatures.)

Magazines

Tropical Fish Hobbyist, TFH Publications, P.O. Box 427, Neptune, New Jersey 07754

Seascope, 8141 Tyler Boulevard, Mentor, Ohio 44060

Aquarium Fish Magazine, P.O. Box 6090, Mission Viejo, CA 92690

Freshwater and Marine Aquarium Magazine, 144 W. Sierra Madre Blvd., Sierra Madre, CA 91024

Internet Sites

www.pbs.org/wgbh/nova/seahorse

www.dragonsearch.asn.au

www.oceanrider.com
   A source for farmed seahorses and supplies.

www.seaponys.com
   A source for dwarf seahorses and supplies.

www.seahorse.mcgill.com
   Project Seahorse, an international program of conservation and management initiatives, constitutes the most intensive effort to date in this area. The project also sponsors a unique survey for those who use, harvest or observe seahorses.

Seafarms@aol.com
   Live seahorses and marine plants.

Organizations

Aquarium for Wildlife Conservation,
Brooklyn, New York 11224
718/265-3400
   A facility of the wildlife conservation society, which also operates the Bronx Zoo. In addition to state-of-the-art exhibits, this institution is on the forefront of research and conservation efforts. Membership in the wildlife conservation society includes a magazine, travel opportunities, free admission, and invitations to special events.

American Museum of Natural History,
Central Park West and 79th Street, New York, NY 10024
   One of the world's premiere natural history collections and educational centers, the museum is an invaluable resource for information on fish of all kinds, including seahorses and their relatives.

Frank Indiviglio
fjindiviglio@aol.com
   Consultations, lectures, fieldwork, freelance writing, and review of publications.

The leafy sea dragon (**Phycodurus eques**) *must be seen to be believed.*

American Aquarist Society, 205/386-7687

Brooklyn Aquarium Society, 718/837-4455

Greater City Aquarium Society, 718/846-6984

Long Island Aquarium Society, *www.webnow.com/LIAS*

Seahorse Nature Aquarium, Unit 3, Kings Wharf, The Quay, Exter, Devon EX 4AN, England
Exhibits, conservation initiatives, and a survey of species of British waters.

The Science Development, Inc., 400 Riverside Drive, Suite 4A, New York, New York 10025
Provides science programs, taught by recognized experts, to schools and other organizations.

Coral assists in maintaining high pH and serves well as a hitching post.

The weedy sea dragon has a much larger snout than its seahorse relatives.

Individual variation and color-changing ability greatly complicates seahorse identification. Pictured above and below are two individuals of the same species, the yellow seahorse (**Hippocampus kuda**).

A Note of Warning

A variety of the electrical appliances are necessary if one is to maintain seahorses in captivity, and most of these are capable of causing the serious injury if misused. Please be sure that all the electrical equipment carries the UL symbol and is appropriate for your purposes. You should consult a licensed electrician if you are unsure. Also, always unplug appliances before working with them in any manner.

Use extreme caution when moving an aquarium, and never do so if the tank contains water. Because accidents can occur, you may wish to add water damage coverage to your liability policy. Please keep all fish medications and other chemicals out of the reach of children, and be sure that your aquarium cannot be toppled over by a curiuos child or pet.

Please also remember that seahorses are extremely difficult to maintain in aquariums and that you will be dimming their prospects for survival in the wild if you rush unprepared into a purchase.

Dedication

This book is dedicated to my cousin, Mary Apa, who did so much to nurture my interests under the most unlikely and trying of circumstances. May she find herein some small acknowledgment of my profound gratitude.

Acknowledgments

My mother, Rita Indiviglio (who helped in the manuscript review), and my sister, Susan Schilling, must rely on their own feelings to know their place in all I do, for any words penned here would be woefully inadequate. My dearest Hye Jeong has strengthened my resolve in more ways that she can possibly know. The rest of my family, Marie and Frank Hill, Sam and Ethel Apa, and Barbara, Mike, Michele, Rita, and Barbara Ann Rotunno, have added immensely to any success I might find.

I have long availed myself of the expertise and friendship of the staff at the Bronx Zoo. William Conway, in particular, has provided lifelong inspiration and been most kind in sharing his knowledge and insights.

I also wish to thank my editor, Bob O'Sullivan, for his hard work and our artist, Michelle Earle-Bridges, for her fine line drawings. Finally, thanks are due to the various photographers who contributed their brilliant photos.

Photo Credits

Aaron Norman: 4, 8, 9, 12 (right), 13 (right), 16, 20 (all), 24, 25, 33, 44, 49 (top), 52, 56, 57, 64, 68 (top), 69, 73 (both), 76 (left), 81, 85 (top l, top r), 89, 92 (bottom r), 93 (top r). **Mark Smith:** 5, 12 (left), 13 (left), 68 (bottom), 72 (both), 76 (right), 77, 88, 92 (top), 93 (top l). **Robert J. Goldstein:** 48 (both), 49 (bottom l, bottom r). **Göthel:** 84 (top l). **Carmela Leszczynski:** 2–3, 17, 45, 53, 61, 65, 93 (bottom). **Kahl:** 60, 84 (top r, bottom). **König:** 21, 85 (bottom l). **McConnaughey:** 85 (bottom r). **Nieuwenhuizen:** 80.

Cover Photos

Front, back, and both inside covers by Aaron Norman.

About the Author

Frank Indiviglio's employment in animal-oriented endeavors spans three decades, and has included a 17-year career with the Bronx Zoo/Wildlife Conservation Park, where he currently works as a herpetologist. Mr. Indiviglio has also been associated with the Staten Island Zoo and has taught at Columbia Preparatory School and for Science Development, Inc. He has participated in a wide variety of field studies throughout the hemisphere and has published and lectured extensively. Mr. Indiviglio holds a Master's Degree in conservation biology and Juris Doctorate from St. John's University. His first book for Barron's, *Newts and Salamanders*, was published in 1997.

All inquiries should be addressed to:
Barron's Educational Series, Inc.
250 Wireless Boulevard
Hauppauge, NY 11788
http://www.barronseduc.com

International Standard Book No. 0-7641-1837-4

Library of Congress Catalog Card No. 2001037359

Library of Congress Cataloging-in-Publication Data
Indiviglio, Frank.
    Seahorses / Frank Indiviglio.
        p. cm.
    ISBN 0-7641-1837-4
    1. Sea horses. I. Title.

SF458.S43 I53 2001
639.3'76798—dc21   2001037359

Printed in Hong Kong

9 8 7 6 5 4 3 2 1